Chartres

ÉMILE MÂLE

Chartres

black and white photographs by

PIERRE DEVINOY

colour photographs by

JACQUES NESTGEN, ÉDITIONS FLAMMARION

translated by

SARAH WILSON

ICON EDITIONS

1817

HARPER & ROW, PUBLISHERS, New York
Cambridge, Philadelphia, San Francisco,
London, Mexico City, São Paulo, Sydney

Copyright © 1983 by Flammarion, Paris, for the original French edition.
Copyright © 1983 by Flammarion, Paris, and Harper & Row Publishers, Inc., for the English language edition. All rights reserved. Printed in France. No part of this book may be used or reproduced in any manner whatsoever without written permission except in the case of brief quotations embodied in critical articles and reviews. For information address Harper & Row, Publishers, Inc., 10 East 53rd Street, New York, N. Y. 10022. Published simultaneously in Canada by Fitzhenry & Whiteside Limited, Toronto.

FIRST U.S. EDITION

ISBN : 0-06-435530-6
LIBRARY OF CONGRESS CATALOG NUMBER : 83-47558

Preface

It was only a century ago that Chartres cathedral was first studied as an architectural and spiritual masterpiece. The great fire of 1836 which destroyed the beautiful timberwork of the roof and could have wrecked the whole building aroused the attention of scholars, artists and the French state. They were shocked that the cathedral could have perished without trace. In 1838, M. de Salvandy, as the Minister responsible, decided to entrust the task of making scale record drawings of the cathedral to the skilled artists Lassus, Amaury-Duval and Paul Durand, and that of preparing a description to the archaeologist Didron. From 1840 onwards, a few magnificent architectural drawings and several fine reproductions did appear in a monumental *Atlas*. But after this spirited beginning, slow progress was made and in 1858 the project, still incomplete, was abandoned. Didron was never to write any of the three volumes promised, and the great monograph was reduced to a few rather superficial explanatory notes by Paul Durand in the *Atlas*[1].

But in 1850, Abbé Bulteau, at the time in the service of the cathedral, produced a *Description de la cathédrale de Chartres,* which was brief, but offered the first systematic studies of the statues and the windows. Written with an erudition that was rare for the period, and though containing a few errors, it demonstrated a real comprehension of the works of the past. Abbé Bulteau himself was quick to see the inadequate aspects of his book, and spent the rest of his life revising it. He died in 1882 with the work unfinished. The Archeological Society of the Eure-et-Loir region printed the first two volumes in 1888 ; the third, which focused on the cathedral interiors and windows, was completed by Abbé Brou and published in 1892. The first volume, with its account of the history of the cathedral from its origins to 1876, is of great interest, largely thanks to the documents it reproduces. In the second volume, the cathedral exterior in its entirety is described ; it remains a useful guide to the sculptural complexities at Chartres despite some inaccuracies and unjustified assertions. The third volume adds little to Abbé Bulteau's *Description* of 1850.

Until the last quarter of the 19th century, works on Chartres cathedral had been purely descriptive. Wilhelm Vöge, a German, was the first to study the Portail Royal from an art historical point of view[2]. He made the most perceptive comments on the style of the twelfth century sculptors who worked on the great porch, and he successfully demonstrated their influence on a few other large groups of sculpture in northern France. His mistakes in dating, however, led him to commit two serious errors. Firstly he asserted that the Portail Royal at Chartres was based on the portal of Saint Trophime at Arles ; and consequently he maintained that Chartres portal in its

1. This *Explication des planches* appeared in 1881 in the *Collection des monuments inédits sur l'histoire de France.*
2. W. Vöge, *Die Anfänge des monumentalen Stiles im Mittelalter,* Strasbourg, 1894, 8vo.

turn was the model for the artists of Saint-Denis. This double error was corrected, first, by Robert de Lasteyrie who, in 1902, in a fine article in *Monuments Piot,* proved that the Saint Trophime portal came after that of Chartres, and secondly by Lanore, who showed in a series of remarkable studies published in the *Revue de l'Art chrétien* that the sculptors of the Portail Royal came to Chartres in 1145 from the workshops of Saint-Denis.

The cathedral's history was emerging from obscurity. The early twentieth century was even more enlightening. The archeological excavations directed by Lefêvre-Pontalis in 1901 and 1903 revealed the position of the façade decorated in 1145, and proved that this façade, with its very weak foundations, was taken down a few years later and rebuilt in alignment with the towers. At the same time, other excavations in the crypt directed by René Merlet, led to the discovery of the ancient well of the Saints Forts which had been a place of pilgrimage throughout the Middle Ages, and to the uncovering of a few portions of the ninth century crypt which led to a better understanding of the plan of the Carolingian cathedral[3].

M. Houvet, a keeper of the cathedral, published his admirable *Album* a few years later. The state with all its resources had been unable to tackle the project which he undertook alone. He resolved with unfailing patience to photograph the entire cathedral. He reproduced not only what could be seen, but what an ordinary spectator could scarcely make out. Like a telescope, his camera revealed unknown wonders. Seven volumes of plates present the architecture and the sculpture, three other volumes deal with the stained glass windows. The canon, M. Delaporte, who was able to examine all the windows closely during their reinstallation after the First World War, described them with a commentary in a superb book illustrated with M. Houvet's plates. This new architectural knowledge was a great step forward. Henceforth, the cathedral in all its aspects could be studied in reproduction, individual ensembles could be examined at leisure, the works compared, the masters distinguished, and the first steps taken to trace stylistic developments. The works published on the art of the Middle Ages during succeeding decades are examples of the influence of this fine collection[4].

This short volume attempts to sum up the most recent architectural discoveries. Hypothesis still has its place, of course, for the definitive history of the cathedral has not yet been written. M. Devinoy, an enthusiastic amateur photographer, has provided the fine illustrations. M. Houvet's ten albums with their nine hundred or more plates are obviously more comprehensive, but the views and details essential for understanding Chartres are provided here. The excellent quality of the photographs is striking : M. Devinoy is an artist for whom time has no meaning : he watches for the right moment, he waits for days at a time until the sky clears and brightens if he needs light, or for it to cloud over if he wants dramatic shadows. He knows that a work of art neutral at one moment may later become transfigured, and his camera is prepared for that sudden illumination which brings the artist's thought to life. Photography, which has already contributed so much on a documentary level allows the art historian to penetrate even deeper into a work's meaning, when it becomes an art form in its own right.

3. Bibliographical information is provided later in the footnotes.
4. For example the remarkable books by M. Aubert, *La sculpture française au début de l'époque gothique*, 4to, 1929 ; and by M. P. Vitry, *La sculpture française au temps de Saint Louis*, 4to, 1929, and by Mme Lefrançois-Pillion, *Les sculpteurs français du XIIe siècle*, 1931 and *Les sculpteurs français du XIIIe siècle*, 2nd edition 1931.

1. Fragment of rood screen,
thirteenth century :
the Nativity.

1. Origins

**The well in the crypt.
The Virgo paritura**

Chance discoveries or archeological excavations have shown more than once that Christian sanctuaries have succeeded to pagan ones. Examples are numerous : the remains of the temple of the Bountiful Goddess were discovered beneath the Church of the Major at Arles, the Church of Saint Vincent at Chalon-sur-Saône is on the site of a temple with an altar erected to Mars, the stone slab of a dolmen may still be seen at the entrance to Puy cathedral where the sick would go and lie to be cured of fever. It is clear that the Church in its wisdom decided to respect the sacred character of age-old pre-Christian places of worship. It sufficed to purify them, and consecrate them to the new religion. The Church sanctified the dolmens in this way, crowning them with the sign of the cross ; she rebaptised fountains with the names of saints, and replaced the roadside gods at crossroads with chapels. The same logic may account for the siting of Chartres cathedral.

In the crypt at Chartres a deep well seems to offer a clue to the cathedral's origins. Its waters were reputed to have miraculous powers, and in the Middle Ages, the sick

7

came to drink there in hope of a cure. The story goes that Chartres' first martyrs were thrown headlong into the well by their executioners. Though the Christians pulled them out, the water had acquired healing properties through contact with these sacred bodies, as the name explains : the "Puits des Saints Forts" — "Well of the Strong Saints". The well was filled in during the seventeenth century by the clergy who were hostile to the practices of popular religion, but it was rediscovered in 1901[1], and recognised as an ancient Celtic well. At the same time, a few traces of a pagan sanctuary built nearby were also found. It is thus highly probable that this well had always possessed a religious character, and popular importance long before Christianity appeared in Gaul. One of the Gauls' many cults was devoted to water, reputedly the daughter of the earth and sky. The Christians at Chartres repeated what they had done so frequently in other places : they built a church in a place consecrated to a pagan water cult.

Very often images of protective divinities, called "Mothers" were found in the vicinity of sacred springs of the Gallo-Roman period. They were generally three figures in such images, but often a single figure could be found : a seated female figure with a child in her lap, bearing a striking resemblance to the Virgin of the medieval period.

Certain historians have thought that there could have been a statuette of this type in the pagan sanctuary built near the well at Chartres[2]. On first consideration, this hypothesis would seem to explain one of the most unusual of the legends about Chartres. This story tells how before the birth of the Virgin, a pagan king from the Chartres region, inspired in a mysterious way, had a sculpture made of a Virgin bearing a child with this prophetic inscription : *Virgini pariturae* — 'to the Virgin about to give birth'. In the Middle Ages in the crypt at Chartres, a wooden statue was worshipped, representing the Virgin with the Child in her lap, reputedly the *Virgo paritura* of this ancient tradition. Early engravings[3] demonstrate its resemblance to a Gallo-Roman "Mother" ; thus from a historical point of view the source of the legend may well be a fanciful interpretation of the original ancient statue. Closer examination, however, throws up some objections. A passage in the writings of a monk named Bernard, a former pupil of the school of Chartres, proves that in the eleventh century the Virgin's statue was not in the cathedral. In 1013, Bernard, travelling in the south of France, was astonished and then indignant to find statues of saints in the region, which he compared to idols of Mars or Jupiter[4]. Statuary, which had begun to appear in the south, was still unknown in the north of France, where it would have appeared to be a form of idolatry. Besides, the chroniclers reveal that in 1194 when the cathedral burnt down, the inhabitants of Chartres took pains to discover the fate of the reliquary casket containing the Virgin's Holy Tunic, but none of them mention the statue of the "Virgin great with child", whose fate should have aroused similar concern.

Again, no allusion to the statue of the "Virgin great with child", can be found in documents prior to the end of the fourteenth century. The first reference appears in 1389 in the *Vieille chronique,* and by the sixteenth century the legend had become more elaborate. Around 1525, an erudite chronicler who had read Caesar, announced that the statue was the work of the Druids, whose gatherings were held in the depths of the Carnutes region in the centre of Gaul[5]. Henceforth the Druids' grotto became a popular feature of the crypt. The real vogue for these stories, however, dates from the sixteenth and the seventeenth centuries[6]. The origin of the *Virgo paritura* rests permanently shrouded in mystery.

The Holy Tunic From earliest times, the Virgin was held in particular veneration at Chartres ; this much is certain. In 876, Charles the Bald presented Chartres with an outstandingly precious relic, the Virgin's Holy Tunic. This gift proves that the cathedral was the most

1. By René Merlet — see his article in the Revue archaéologique, 1901.
2. R. Merlet, *La cathédrale de Chartres*, p. 11.
3. The appearance of the statue, burned during the Revolution, is known through old engravings and a copy at the Carmelite monastery of Bergen-op-Zoom in Holland.
4. *Miracula Sanctae Fidis* Lib. 1, cap XIII, ed. A. Bouillet.
5. See R. Merlet, *Rev. archéol.,* 1902, vol. II, p. 432, and Jusselin Mém. de la Soc. arch. d'Eure-et-Loir, vol. XV, 1914.
6. Sébastien Rouillard, in his *Parthénie* 1609, further embellished these anecdotes by introducing the reader into the Druid gatherings. The great vogue for Druids at the time is demonstrated by Honoré d'Urfé's *Astrée*.

celebrated centre of the cult of the Virgin in northern France during the Carolingian period. The tunic had been sent from the Emperor of Byzantium to Charlemagne, who added it to the treasures of his palace chapel at Aix-la-Chapelle. The Middle Ages boasted no relic more pure or more poetic than this tunic, worn by the Virgin at the moment of the Annunciation. From very early on, Chartres considered the Holy Tunic as a defence and a pledge of safety. It had been in the cathedral but a few years when Rollon, still a pagan, came and laid siege to the town in 911. An eleventh century chronicler tells how during the battle the bishop of Chartres appeared on the city walls, waving the Holy Tunic like a standard. The Normans, filled with terror at the sight, panicked, broke ranks and fled. Rollon, having personally experienced the power of Notre-Dame de Chartres, hastened to make her a gift. According to the symbols of pagan custom, a little knife held on a silken cord was attached to the parchment recording the gift. With an epic grandeur and brevity, the donor had dictated the following words : "I, Rollon, Duke of Normandy, give to the brotherhood of the church Notre-Dame de Chartres my castle at Malmaison, which I took with my sword, and with my sword I shall be their guarantor. May this knife be my witness."

The Holy Tunic was Chartres' great relic, the source of the cathedral's fame and position as a focal point for pilgrims through the centuries. The highly precious relic was locked away in a reliquary casket of cedarwood, which, towards the end of the tenth century, had been covered with gold by a goldsmith named Teudon. Each generation added its ornaments, and suspended precious objects from its four sides. Antique cameos could be seen hanging there ; the most beautiful, donated by Charles V, represented Jupiter, not Saint John as was originally believed because of his eagle[7]. On a background strewn with rubies, topazes and amethysts, two eagles worked in gold stood out, formerly engraved by Saint Eloi. King Robert's gift was an enormous sapphire, and a gold enamelled griffin was brought back from the East at the time of the crusades. Philip the Handsome left a ruby there, and the Duc de Berry left badges inlaid with his arms. The small Virgin crowned by two angels was the one Louis XI wore on his hat, and Anne of Brittany presented the golden belt encircling the casket. Innumerable roses in enamel, crowns, flowers, golden castles, letters of precious stones and pearls forming the Virgin's name, made up the gifts from anonymous donors. A large number of other offerings had to be placed in the three cathedral treasuries, there being no more room on the reliquary itself. Some were magnificent, others of a touching naivety, like the porcupine-skin belt bordered in silks sent by the Huron tribe, and the eleven thousand porcelain beads (representing the number of inhabitants in the country) offered by the Abenaquis tribe of New France. The gifts did not cease until the eve of the French Revolution[8]. This highly precious, much venerated reliquary, was never opened, and the Holy Tunic remained invisible for centuries. Not even the sovereign was allowed to see it, and when Henry IV, consecrated at Chartres in 1594, insisted, he was informed that the keys could not be found.

As the Virgin's Tunic remained a mystery it assumed the form of a shirt in the popular imagination, and was often called "the holy shirt". In the fifteenth century a leaden hat-badge bearing an image of the shirt was worn by pilgrims coming to Chartres. Small copies of the shirt in metal were pressed against the reliquary, and were then worn by soldiers as protective amulets. In a duel, the gentleman who bore a "little shirt" from Chartres on his chest, was duty bound to warn this adversary of the fact. Linen shirts, brought into contact with the casket, helped women to bear the pains of childbirth — the queens of France included.

When the Revolution arrived, the casket was opened, and the Holy Tunic was revealed, violating the mystery. Far from resembling a shirt, it was one of those lengths of cloth used by eastern women to drape themselves. It was accompanied by a veil decorated with lions in combat. On consulting the learned Abbé Barthélemy it was revealed that these materials were Syrian in origin, and could well date back to the first century A.D. Today, only a few fragments of the Tunic and the veil saved during the Terror remain enshrined in a modern reliquary.

The Well, the Holy Tunic and later the statue in the crypt made Chartres unique. This was the great centre of worship for the Virgin : the cathedral appeared to be her

7. It may be seen today in the Cabinet des Médailles.
8. See F. De Mely, *Le trésor de Chartres,* 1886, and L. Merlet, *Catalogue des reliques et joyaux de Notre-Dame de Chartres,* 1885.

dwelling place on earth. At Chartres, when the hymn "O gloriosa" was sung in her honour, all the verbs were given in the present tense, to demonstrate her presence[9]. The Virgin's abode had to be as pure as herself : while other churches were full of tombs, not a single one was found at Chartres cathedral. The great fête-days in honour of Notre-Dame were celebrated by crowds filling her church both day and night, trampling the fresh herbs strewn underfoot. On the morrow it was purified, by letting water stream over the pavement which was designed to slope slightly for this purpose. At Chartres, the slightest things evoked the presence of Notre-Dame : for example the chapter of canons insisted on virgin wax for sealing its annals. Notre-Dame de Chartres inspired the ancient orders of chivalry in France, who demonstrated their fervour by donating stained glass windows, gifts offered to the cathedral by the great feudal families. More than one warrior-knight made her name his battle cry[10]. Vows were made to her during battle, and the Sire de Coucy kept his last thought for her as he lay dying in Brousse, a prisoner of the Moslems[11]. The great events of French history found their echo in her church. In 1304, after the victory of Mons-en-Puelle, Philip the Handsome gave his war armour and his helmet crowned with golden lilies as an offering to Notre-Dame[12]. In 1328, Philippe de Valois, victorious at Mont Cassel, appeared in arms and on horseback at the cathedral door. He offered his horse and his armour to the Virgin in homage, and having redeemed them, donated their price to the church. In 1360, prior to the treaty of Bretigny, Edward III, the victorious king of England, who already called himself "King of France" proposed to conquer the entire country. As he approached Chartres cathedral with his army, a storm broke out of such violence that he understood the Virgin's hostility to his plans, and her defence of the cause of her defeated people.

Chartres had a powerful sway over the imagination, and the effect could be astonishing. The great building projects of the twelfth century and the reconstruction of the thirteenth century were undertaken in this climate of popular enthusiasm. As a study of the foundations in the crypt shows, the various cathedrals which succeeded one another on the same site grew progressively more vast, along with the cult of the Virgin. The ninth century church was of modest proportions, but it already had an ambulatory, a plan which allowed the congregation to walk around the choir, eminently suitable for a pilgrimage church. In the eleventh century, this ambulatory, enlarged by the illustrious bishop Fulbert, opened into three radiating chapels ; the church itself grew larger, as the dimensions of the two long vaulted galleries of the crypt indicate. In the twelfth century it was lengthened again, while the noble proportions admired today were finally achieved in the thirteenth century, the addition of the transept and the porches becoming with time more spacious, more worthy of Notre-Dame.

9. Sébastien Rouillard, *Parthénie*, vol. I, p. 164.
10. Cahier and Martin, *Mélanges d'archéologie*, vol. 1, pp. 51 ff.
11. *Mém. de la Société d'Eure-et-Loir*, vol. IX, p. 463.
12. The king's coat of mail and his helmet, bereft of its golden lilies, are now in the Musée de Chartres.

2. Fragment of rood screen,
thirteenth century.

2. The twelfth century cathedral

Chartres cathedral in the form it is today dates back to the twelfth century, at which time the old cathedral built by Fulbert in the first years of the eleventh century and restored by Saint Ives was still standing, but was beginning to seem inadequate[1]. The heroic generations of the Crusaders had a feeling for grandeur. Just before the middle of the twelfth century, it was decided that a bell-tower should be built some distance away from the façade. The idea of a steeple or bell-tower conceived as a building on its own, unconnected with the rest of the church, was still current in the twelfth century, as it had been in much earlier times, and this was the origin of the design of the northern steeple, which Jean de Beauce completed in the sixteenth century with a Gothic spire in the flamboyant style[2].

1. It did, however, have a tower on his façade, which formed a porch at ground floor level. This was proven by the archeological excavation undertaken by the architect M. Trouvelot and the core-samples taken by M. Fels. See M. Marcel Aubert's article : *Le portail royal et la façade de la cathédrale de Chartres* in the *Bulletin monumental* of 1941.
2. Windows, which today open into the church and are redundant, prove that the steeple once stood on its own.

Soon however, a desire for symmetry led to the erection of a complementary tower of similar design on the southern side. Then it was decided that the two steeples should no longer be isolated, but united with the cathedral which was therefore extended to reach them : finally the decision was taken to build in front of the old eleventh century façade a new and more magnificent façade adorned with sculpture, which would be truly worthy of Notre-Dame.

This façade was recessed between the two steeples, which framed it with their strong soaring lines and cast shadows which threw the statues into a half-light, enhancing their mystery. Such was the original state of the new façade. As we shall shortly see, it was brought forward a few years later and rebuilt in alignment with the towers.

Popular enthusiasm for the cathedral

These tall spires, rising up in honour of Notre-Dame, inspired an extraordinary degree of fervour in the Chartres region. This incredible popular enthusiasm is attested to by several contemporary eyewitness accounts, which reveal something of the genius of the twelfth century, one of the great centuries of French history.

In 1144, Robert de Torigni, the Abbot of Mont-Saint-Michel wrote in his *Chronique* : "That year at Chartres people could be seen harnessed to wagons loaded with stones, wood, wheat, everything which could advance the work on the cathedral, whose towers were rising as if by magic. The enthusiasm spread to Normandy and the Ile de France : everywhere you could see men and women dragging heavy loads across the marshy plains ; everywhere people were doing penance, everywhere people were forgiving their enemies[3]". Robert de Torigni is correct when he assures us that it was Chartres which set the example. A letter written the following year by Haimon, Abbot of Saint-Pierre-sur-Dives confirms this account in every detail. He tells the English monks of Tutbury about the extraordinary events happening before his eyes in Normandy. Brotherhoods, he said, were being formed, imitating the one which had been formed at Chartres cathedral. Thousands of the faithful could be seen, men and women harnessed to heavy wagons laden with all the labourers could need, wood, lime, corn, oil. These volunteers included powerful lords and ladies of noble birth. Perfect discipline and a profound silence reigned among them. During the night, they formed a camp with their wagons, and by the light of candles, they sang canticles and psalms. They brought their sick with them, hoping that they would be cured. Peace and harmony were established. If someone was so hard at heart that he could not forgive his enemies, his offering was taken off the wagon as defiled, and he was chased from the saintly company in disgrace[4].

In that same year of 1145, a letter from Hugues, archbishop of Rouen, to Thierry, bishop of Amiens recounted absolutely similar events. He told him that the Normans who had heard what was happening at Chartres had visited the site and come back resolved to imitate what they had seen. They formed themselves into groups, and having confessed their sins, they harnessed themselves to wagons, with a leader to direct them. The archbishop adds : "We allowed our bishops to go and practice this form of devotion in other dioceses[5]". This valuable passage proves that many other churches whose names remain unknown were built in this manner. The creative output of the twelfth century was prodigious. In France there are vast regions where there is hardly a village church which does not date back to the twelfth century. It is quite astonishing just how much talent, labour and resources were required to achieve this immense task. There was a blossoming of faith at the time, a spirit of sacrifice and abnegation whose finest symbol remains the building of the twin spires of Chartres.

The twelfth century steeples

The first sight to greet the visitor to Chartres cathedral is the twelfth century façade. Of the many outstanding works in France that date from this century, none are more beautiful than the sculptures on the three portals and the southern steeple[6]. The

3. *Monum. Germ. Script.*, vol. VI, p. 496.
4. Haimon's letter was published for the first time by Leopold Delisle, *Biblioth. de l'École de Chartres*, fifth series, vol. I.
5. *Patrol. lat.*, vol. CXCII, Col. 1135.
6. It is the one to the spectator's right, since Chartres' main axis runs from east to west.

northern steeple remained incomplete for a long time and did not receive its spire until the sixteenth century, but the southern steeple was built all of a piece, and remained unequalled throughout the Romanesque period.

There are many others, however, which are magnificent in their own way. The steeples of Saint-Germain d'Auxerre and of the Trinité de Vendôme which the architect of Chartres would have known, are similar in type, but not so perfect. The main lines of the design are the same : a quadrangular tower with three divisions, which from the fourth storey upwards becomes octagonal, with a spire jutting from the octagon. Pinnacles crown the four angles left free where the octagon begins, and tall dormer-windows are cut into the faces turned towards the four cardinal points. At Chartres, these dormer-windows and these pinnacles surrounded by tall, thin gables skilfully conceal the passage from the square to the octagonal sections, and surround the base of the spire. The transition between the square tower and the polygonal spire is imperceptible ; the resulting continuity of spirit and impression of unity are not found elsewhere. As for the spire, its beauty remains unparalleed. The steeple which forms its base is sixty metres high and the spire itself rises to a height of 105 metres, with no ornament other than the structural ribs and the overlapping tiles which accentuate the upward movement. There are no decorative crockets on the ridges as with the spires of the following period, and no trefoil or quatre-foil openings cut into the sheer, heavy face of the pyramid. It has a grandiose simplicity and a confidence and pride which make it unique as a monument, one of the masterpieces of the art of the Middle Ages. For well-nigh eight hundred years it has braved tempests and thunderbolts. It is only eighty centimetres thick at the base and thirty centimetres thick at the summit, but its stones were assembled with such perfection that they seem to have the solidity of metal. Assailed from the outside by strong winds, it was beset from within by the stormy peal of bells ; eighteen men were necessary to set each one of the great bells in motion. The wooden framework which bore their weight burnt down twice, but the inner walls of the tower, blackened and charred on the surface have lost none of their solidity. The tall pyramid terminates in an iron cross, surmounted by a crescent moon, for it is on a crescent moon that the Woman of the Apocalypse rests her feet. The Gothic spire of the other tower bears an image of the sun on its cross to remind us that the Woman of the Apocalypse was dressed in rays of light. In his mind's eye, the imaginative worshipper could see the Virgin looking down from on high above the steeples of Chartres.

The spire, here developed to the point of perfection, is an invention of Northern France. The southern regions, faithful to classical designs, scarcely used it at all. In Gothic architecture, the spire was a sign of those vast aspirations which would soon be given expression in the building of naves. The northern French provinces, like those of the centre, are passionately fond of spires. Each village wanted its own. Seen from far away this tall symbol simultaneously aroused a love of one's native land, and pointed towards another world.

The west façade   The façade is pierced by three portals which are unique in that all three give access to the nave. It is obvious that the towers were being built in the extension of the two side aisles when the construction of the portals was undertaken : thus they could only take up the width of the nave. They are also narrower in width than the portals of other French cathedrals, which generally correspond to divisions within the interior[7]. Though the portals at Chartres may be small, they are imposing in their elaborate conception and the richness of architectural detail.

The portal to the right of the spectator represents what was known in the Middle Ages as the First Coming of Jesus Christ, in other words his appearance on earth. The son of God was born of a Virgin, and the Mother and her Son are glorified simultaneously. The left portal shows the Saviour's mission ending with his earthly life. He rises to the heavens while angels proclaim to the apostles that their Master will return when time has run full circle. This Second Coming fills the central portal. Christ appears as the God of the Apocalypse on the last day of the world. He is accompanied by the twenty-four Elders of the Apocalypse and the four symbolic beasts. He is now the Judge

7. Except for Notre-Dame de Paris, where there are only three portals for five interior divisions ; but at Bourges, where there is also a nave with double side aisles, there are five portals.

of mankind, and the apostles seated on the lintel assist him in judgment. The history of the world achieves fulfilment.

This imposing summary of God's appearances on earth would not be complete without a place for the humanity he has come to save. It is represented, in fact, on the voussoirs of the arches. Humanity appears condemned to the law of labour, but as the theologians taught, labour was associated with man's work for redemption.

During the Middle Ages, work had only two aspects. In the first place, every month of the year witnessed man's constant struggle with nature, and the grand cycle of sowing, reaping and the wine harvest can be seen on the voussoirs of the left portal. Secondly comes the struggle of the spirit to conquer truth, and on the voussoirs of the right portal the seven sciences of the Trivium and the Quadrivium are depicted, embodied as the seven Muses, escorted by the great men who celebrate their virtues.

The complex systems of thought of the twelfth century theologians are revealed in these three tympana and their voussoirs, but the accompanying statues suggest even broader perspectives. They represent the characters of the Old Testament who are the ancestors of Jesus Christ in the flesh, or his precursors in spirit. The Old Law leads towards the New, and the Bible serves as the gateway to the Gospel. The Gospel itself

4. Portail Royal.
Tympanum, central bay.
Christ in majesty
surrounded by the symbols
of the four apostles.
Angels and the Elders
of the Apocalypse.
Apostles.

15

unfurls in a continuous frieze above the heads of the biblical statues, on the capitals which crown the three portals. In this way the harmony of history and the unity of divine thought is revealed. No church façade before this had expressed such elevated themes or so clearly summed up the drama of the Redemption. Here one can appreciate that Chartres was then one of the great schools of theology in France. A slender statue, standing at the angle of the southern tower adds a final touch to the magnificent western façade. An angel holds a large sundial against her breast while shadows move across it[8]. This grave and gentle figure seems to tell the passer-by that each hour is a gift from God, and is brought to him by an angel.

5. Portail Royal.
Figure in the embrasure
of the left bay.

Origins of the art of Chartres. The work of Suger at Saint-Denis

This initial impression must now give way to a detailed study. The first question concerns the origins of the artists who were capable of such an impressive creation. The art of these sculptors is already so refined that their training poses a mystery which is only now approaching a solution.

During the first half of the twelfth century, the reconstruction and decoration of the Abbey of Saint-Denis by Suger was the greatest architectural achievement in Northern France. The project was completed in 1144, when the abbey was consecrated. The Gothic choir could then be seen in all its beauty, and for the first time a portal was created, decorated with a sculpted tympanum, storiated voussoirs and tall statues. So the Gothic portal was invented at Saint-Denis in the twelfth century and it was imitated

8. This statue of an angel dates from the twelfth century. It was originally one of the statues of the Portail royal who announced the Messiah. It was doubtless in the sixteenth century that she was placed in the angle of the tower and received wings and a sundial.

6. Spire
of the Romanesque tower.

in various European countries as the architectural triumph of the thirteenth century. Suger allows us some insight into his creation in revealing that he had summoned artists to Chartres from various regions of France[9]. He does not say where these sculptors came from, it is true, but certain suppositions are very probably correct.

The central portal of the façade at Saint-Denis was mutilated during the Revolution and disgracefully restored in 1839, thus losing its qualities as a work of art, and blurring questions of style, although the broad lines of the design and the subject matter remain perfectly distinct. The Christ of the Last Judgment, bare-breasted, and with arms outstretched, stands before his cross. A very similar Christ appears in fact in the south of France, on the portal at Beaulieu[10], sculpted a few years previously[11]. Other influences from the south may also be observed. One of the great beauties of this Saint-Denis portal was the series of statues aligned on either side of the doorway apparently granting access to the sanctuary. These statues have disappeared, but are shown in Montfaucon's drawings[12]. Some possessed rather peculiar features : their legs were curiously crossed together as though about to break into a dance. This feature was quite characteristic of the old School of Toulouse. As at Toulouse one of the Saint-Denis figures wears a skullcap with two flaps on his head : its only precedent may be found in southern France. But there are even more clues. A few years ago, at the Musée de Toulouse a portal was reconstructed from the chapter house of the cloister at Saint-Etienne dating from the first years of the twelfth century. The various fragments had been kept, but the effect, once reassembled, could not have been imagined. It was a great surprise to see the apostles stand flanking the portal in the splays. They were not statues, it is true, but very prominent bas-reliefs ; nevertheless, the total effect was already that of a Gothic portal — not very daring and extremely incomplete, as there was no tympanum or storiated voussoirs — but the broad outlines were there. These parallels suggest that Suger's sculptors must have come from the south of France. They were trained at the beginning of the twelfth century in the great school which produced masterpiece upon masterpiece at Toulouse, Moissac, Beaulieu, Carennac, Souillac and Cahors. The sculptors surpassed themselves in response to Suger's demanding and noble imagination : as the tympanum took shape, the voussoirs came to life alive with figures, and the bas-reliefs, which at Toulouse flanked either side of the portal, turned at Saint-Denis into statues leaning against columns. These were not the apostles, but figures from the Old Testament, revealing Suger's paramount genius as a thinker. It was doubtless Suger who saw the Bible as the gateway to the Gospel, one of his favourite ideas, and this is proved by the stained-glass windows where he dictated the subject matter to the artists personally.

Saint-Denis was finished in 1144, when the steeples at Chartres were being built, and the preparations for the great façade were in hand. The bishop of Chartres at the time was Geoffroy de Lèves, a friend of Suger, who was evidently interested in his project. He followed its progress on his several journeys to Saint-Denis, and celebrated Mass there on the very day that violent storm broke out, as Suger has described[13]. The vaults near the altar had not yet met overhead, only the skeleton of diagonal ribs had been constructed. Terrified, Geoffroy de Lèves saw these ribs move to and fro above his head with the force of the wind ; but they did not give way, and the structural principle of this new architecture gave ample proof of its excellence that day. This explains the diagonal rib constructions in both towers of Chartres cathedral. In 1144, Geoffroy de Lèves was one of the prelates who came from every part of the kingdom to the consecration of the Abbey of Saint-Denis. This was no doubt the occasion when, admiring Suger's church in all its beauty, he resolved to summon to Chartres the artists whose work at Saint-Denis had just been completed.

7. West facade.

9. *Liber de rebus in administratione sua gestis.* Ed. Lecoy de la Marche.
10. In the Corrèze department of France.
11. I have made these comparisons with more details in *L'Art religieux du XIIe siècle en France*, pp. 178 ff.
12. *Monum. de la Monarchie française*, vol. I, pp. 194 ff. Pl. XVI, XVII, XVIII.
13. Suger, *Libellus de Consecratione*, ch. VI, VII.

8. West facade,
rose window.

9. West facade.
Portals and triplet.

10. Romanesque tower.
    Tower base.

11. Romanesque tower.
    Springing of spire.

**The statues
of the west façade
or the "Portail royal"**

There is a striking resemblance between the statues of the west portal at Chartres, generally known as the Portail royal, and the statues at Saint-Denis, as they appear in Montfaucon's drawings. The costumes are the same, the attitudes very similar, the figures, equally rigid, have their arms pressed to their bodies and carry books or scrolls held tightly against their chests. These statues, with their marked similarity, must be identical in meaning. These kings and queens, these high priests with their Jewish skullcaps could only be figures from the Old Testament, ancestors or precursors of Christ. The queen we see between two kings is perhaps Bathsheba, wife of David and mother of Solomon, or perhaps the Queen of Sheba, who was received by Solomon[14]. It is certain, however, that the figure wearing the Jewish skullcap and carrying the broken tablets of the Law is Moses[15]. Here at Chartres, as it did at Saint-Denis the Old Testament gives way to the New.

Careful examination of these statues at Chartres reveals the hands of several artists. The greatest is the master of the tall figures of the central portal[16]. On the left portal, three statues with drapery in circular folds have a spirit so different that they could almost come from a different school. The sculptor, whose work is so distinct from all that surrounds it, was probably trained in Bourgogne, for similar circular folds, though finer in quality, are found only on the tympanum at Vézelay[17].

On the right portal the presence of a pupil of the principal sculptor is seen, in three figures on the left side, while to the right, three statues with prominent eyes are the work of a different artist.

The school of sculpture at Chartres thus had several artists as members, each with his own temperament, but they were not the only ones : there were others as well, whose work may be appreciated through study of the tympana and the voussoirs.

The designer of the central portal was one of the great sculptors of the Chartres school. He alone had the idea of turning the statues into columns, an original idea which was only suggested at Saint-Denis, if Montfaucon's drawing are taken as a guide. Not only did he elongate his figures out of all proportion, but he omitted the usual canopy over their heads, thus ensuring that the column was uninterrupted in its movement ; the pedestals were also reduced as much as possible. The gathered folds are vertical, the arms, brought up against the chest, hold the books vertically ; the broad outlines rise up in parallel towards the capitals. Conceived in this way, the statues unite harmoniously with the architecture, becoming a functional part of it. The male figures sculpted by this remarkable artist have a nobility and highly idealised character which already looks forward to the great art of the thirteenth century. His female figures, however, are true marvels, and here his talent is given full scope. They are even taller than the male ones, and seem like actual columns, fluted with innumerable grooves. In one of his letters, Poussin expresses the charming idea that the columns at the Maison Carrée used the beautiful young girls of Nîmes for models. He imagined women transformed into columns — here we see columns metamorphosed into women. The Greeks did the same for the Cnidian treasury at Delphi and the Erechtheion at Athens, more imposingly, but with less magic. Here one is no longer in the world of goddesses, but the kingdom of fairyland. These vaguely smiling courtly ladies emanate a strange poetry, the poetry of Breton lays, soon to become the romances of the Round Table. They are dressed in long robes gathered into finely pleated bodices, and cloaks with huge sleeves. One of them has tresses which descend almost to her knees, others have belts whose tasselled ends hang almost to the ground. This costume, one of the most queenly ever worn by woman, consists wholly of vertical lines, giving an impression of greater height. It is the apparel of Eleanor of Acquitaine and the noble ladies of the troubadour songs. This is how they appeared in courtly gatherings at Troyes, Provins, or in the Orient, at Antioch or Tripoli. The sculptor has studied every detail of their dress with loving care, but his astonishing exactitude in no way spoils the dream. These tall figures seem like apparitions about to grow even taller before dissolving into smoke. They seem so strange, so distant, that one can well imagine from their faces Bathsheba or the

14. This queen standing between two kings may be found again on the portal of Le Mans cathedral, in open imitation of the one at Chartres. Apparently in 1841 the name of Solomon could still be read on the reliquary one of the kings was holding.
15. Moses is also seen at Saint-Denis.
16. To these must be added the Moses of the left portal.
17. The same artist sculpted the statues on the portal of the church of Notre-Dame at Étampes. The statues on the portal, now destroyed, at the Madeleine at Châteaudun were also by his hand or from his workshop.

Queen of Sheba herself. One has only to compare the charming, sensible young queen of the northern portal[18] sculpted around 1220 with these fairy queens of 1145 to realise the difference which separates a talented artist from a true poet.

The right portal represents Christ's First Coming, in other words the beginning of his earthly life. The two lintels are taken up with scenes from the Annunciation, the Visitation, the Nativity, the Adoration of the Shepherds, and the Presentation to the Temple. During these first days of the Redemption, the Virgin is not yet separated from her Son and there is an evident desire to honour her at the same time as her Child. These two lintels are the work of two new sculptors. The first, who carved the Presentation at the Temple, characteristically uses features from much earlier styles : disproportionate heads, too large for their bodies, and rigid figures lined up behind each other. The artist aimed to animate the faces by boring holes into the pupils of the eyes. The second artist carved the Annunciation, the Visitation, the Nativity and the Adoration of the Shepherds. He shows a much more accurate sense of proportion and he has some very

**The right portal :
tympanum and voussoirs**

18. It is on the right hand portal of the north façade.

felicitious ideas : witness the naive shepherd trying to play a carol on his pan-pipes, or the Virgin lying on her bed in meditation with her hand on her cheek[19].

The true master, however, reveals himself on the tympanum. The imposing figure of the Virgin bearing the Child, with two angels wafting incense over her, is his work. The Virgin appears here for the first time in this place of honour. In view of the devout cult in her honour at Chartres, nothing would seem more natural. Majestically seated on her throne, crowned and dressed in a long robe with beautiful folds, she bears the Child, who sits facing outwards on her knees. As the Middle Ages would have it, she is literally the Throne of the Almighty. An even more solemn effect was given by a canopy, of which only the column's base remains. Two angels with censers in their hands lightly move towards her, their tunics fluttering. Since 431 AD, when the council of Ephesus pronounced the divinity of motherhood, the Virgin had been represented with a supernatural grandeur in Oriental mosaics, but contemporary sculpture had attempted nothing similar. The superhuman Virgin of Chartres, majestic as befits a profound theological idea, and the whole group picked out in gold[20], is the first to be seen on a church tympanum in France. Regrettably, the two faces, eroded by time, seem veiled today ; the Virgin's expression, eyes raised to the sky, is scarcely visible. Documentary

13. Portail Royal, capitals. Left bay, left side. The Life of Christ : Massacre of the Innocents.

19. M. Marcel Aubert, in the *Bulletin Monumental* article quoted above supposes that the two portals on the left and right were originally smaller, with only one lintel apiece. The lintels showing the Presentation at the Temple on the right, and to the left, the four angels speaking to the apostles at the moment of the Ascension, would have been added later. It is an ingenious hypothesis but certain difficulties stand in its way.

evidence gives a date for this masterpiece of before 1150, because Richard, Archdeacon of Chateaudun who bore the expenses, died in that year.

This Virgin conceived so elaborately was worthy of the school of theology and philosophy at Chartres. This school was old, but its fame dates from the beginning of the eleventh century and the teachings of Fulbert who was called "that venerable Socrates" by his disciples. The twelfth century marked the zenith of the Chartres School. Bernard of Chartres, Gilbert de la Porée, Thierry of Chartres, and John of Salisbury, who were its masters and were celebrated throughout France, attracted pupils from every province, even from abroad[21]. Chartres was at once a town of holy mysteries and a town of learning ; the praises of Notre-Dame were sung there and commentaries on Aristotle's *Organum* were written. For his pupils Thierry of Chartres composed his *Heptateuchon,* a treatise on the seven liberal arts, while the cathedral portals were being sculpted. In addition, the designer of the portals, possibly Geoffroy de Levès himself, imitating Suger's fervour, wished to see the seven arts portrayed on the voussoirs of the Virgin's portal. The human sciences, taught for the glory of Notre-Dame in the School, were personified as her retinue on the cathedral façade. The angels surrounding the Virgin form the first arch of the voussoirs, the seven Arts, personified by seven female figures, form the second. These seven Muses are firstly

14. Portail Royal, capitals. Left bay, right side. The Life of Christ : Annunciation to the shepherds, the Magi.

20. *Cartulaire de N.-D. de Chartres,* vol. III, p. 19 : *"Decoravit introitum hujus ecclesiae imaginae beatae Mariae auro decenter ornata".*
21. See Clerval, *Les Écoles de Chartres au Moyen Âge,* 1895.

those of the Trivium : Grammar, Rhetoric and Dialectic ; then those of the Quadrivium : Arithmetic, Geometry, Astronomy and Music. These seven great divisions of human knowledge date back to antiquity. Martianus Capella, an African master of rhetoric at the end of the classical period, first had the idea of personifying these mother-sciences. In the *Noces de Mercure et de la Philologie* he describes them, and their dress, their attributes, and the retinue of great men, whose fame derived from them. Martianus Capella's book captivated the Middle Ages, and his allegories were borrowed by poets as well as artists[22].

Their first appearance in a monumental art of this scale was at Chartres, an honour appropriate for the most famous theological school in France before the creation of the University of Paris. In contrast to those of Martianus Capella, these Muses appear considerably simplified : for the most part they are bereft of the ornaments and attributes with which he overburdened them, but in accordance with the ancient rhetorician each is accompanied by one of the great men who interpreted their arts.

Grammar, a cane in her hand, teaches two children to read, with Priscian or perhaps Donatus at her feet. Cicero accompanies Rhetoric who makes an orator's gesture and Aristotle accompanies Dialectic, who bears a dragon-headed serpent on her knees, symbol of the sinuous paths of thought. Pythagoras (unless perhaps it is Boethius), is seen together with Arithmetic, whose attribute has disappeared ; Euclid accompanies Geometry, drawing her diagrams on a tablet, Ptolemy is with Astronomy, whose head

15. Portail Royal, capitals. Central bay. The Life of Christ : *from right to left :* **Marriage of the Virgin, the Visitation.**

22. I have studied Martianus Capella's influence in *L'art religieux du XIIIe siècle en France*, book II.

is tilted back to gaze at the stars, and finally Pythagoras comes with Music, who strikes small bells with a hammer. Thus Chartres expressed its respect for classical antiquity, mother of the sciences. A few years before, Bernard, a canon and one of the principal teachers, had written these surprising lines : "If we see further than the ancients it is not thanks to our strength of sight, but because they elevate us, raising us to a prodigious height. We are dwarfs standing on the shoulders of giants"[23]. Such was the extent of the regard for antiquity in the School of Chartres, where, howerer, the *Physics* or *Metaphysics* of Aristotle remained unknown and Plato was known only by a Latin translation of his *Thimaeus*.

The voussoirs which surround the tympanum have all been attributed to the master who sculpted the Virgin. Some of the figures of angels, of the Sciences personified and of the philosophers, with their very distinguishable, elegant lines, are indeed very possibly by his hand, but the erosion is such that this remains uncertain. Some very well preserved figures of learned men and the Sciences, however, are works of quite another style and temper ; they are both strongly accentuated and very sensitively observed. Aristotle's likeness is a small masterpiece : seated with a desk on his knees, he holds his scraper in one hand, while the other plunges his pen into a brimming inkhorn ; his brow is wrinkled with meditation, and before drawing out his pen, he appears to brood over the thought he will cast on the parchment. His head seems excessively large, if one fails to observe that only half his body is represented.

23. Quoted by John of Salisbury in his *Métalogique*, III, 4. Patrol. lat., vol. CXCIX, col. 900.

16. Portail Royal, capitals.
Central bay.
The Life of Christ :
from right to left :
The bathing of Mary at her birth,
Mary visits the temple
with her parents,
Mary and Joseph
married by the high priest.

The left portal : tympanum and voussoirs

On the left portal, Christ, his earthly life completed, rises to the heavens in the presence of his apostles. A curtain of cloud, a sort of falling garland, its ends held by angels, already separates him from the world. These angels swoop down in a gracious movement towards the apostles, to reveal that their Master will reappear on the last day. A perfect symmetry is maintained between this Ascension portal and the portal of the Virgin. The divisions are identical, and it is to complement the dimensions of the seated Virgin that Christ, though standing, is not completely full-length. Without hesitation the two tympana must be attributed to the same master.

Certain singular features betray the origins of this great sculptor. Doubtless he came straight from Saint-Denis, but his education had been completed in the south of France. Bearing the many parallels in mind, he must have seen the portal at Collonges in the Corrèze region, where Christ rises above a wavy line of clouds held by two angels like a piece of drapery. Above all, however, he knew the Ascension at Cahors ; there are no clouds there, it is true, but on either side of Christ, angels, turned to face the apostles, stretch out forming two arcs, the movement imitated with a few proportional adjustments by the sculptor at Chartres[24]. Had time not caused such erosion, a reflection of the beautiful Christ at Cahors (bearing the stamp of divinity on his noble face) would probably be recognisable at Chartres. But the four angels of Cahors are rediscovered here, throwing themselves down from the heavenly heights to meet their God. At Chartres, however, to fill up one of the lintels, they had to be placed between Christ and the apostles. The apostles themselves, the work of a pupil, are close in

17. Portail Royal, capitals.
Central bay, right side.
The Life of Christ :
The Last Supper,
Saint Peter cuts off
Malchus' ear,
Judas betrays Christ.

attributes, though not in style, to the apostles at Carennac in the Lot region. They are similarly seated and often have their legs crossed in the same southern manner. Thus the influence of south-eastern France, so much in evidence at Saint-Denis, is once more recognisable at Chartres.

It is tempting to attribute the voussoirs to the sculptor of the tympanum, as those which are still visible, and those whose outlines remain, are full of charm[25]. The portrayals of the rhythms of the seasons, together with the signs of the zodiac are unsurpassed in the pure poetry of their lifelike depiction. The gestures shown are wonderfully apt. The thresher in the barn bends over to part his sheaves before seizing the flail, cast aside on the straw ; one man picks grapes, while another empties his full basket into the vat. The peasant raises his axe above the pig who is munching peacefully unaware, his snout in the trough. Thus, the timeless peasant with his age-old gestures appears side by side with the imposing images of the Virgin and of Christ, not far from the prophetic figures of the kings and queens of the Bible. The sculpture at Chartres is supremely rich in form and spirit ; still close to its origins, it dares at this early date to express both the mysteries of the heavens and the realities of earthly life.

18. Portail Royal, capitals. Central bay, right side. The Life of Christ : Judas betrays Christ, the Entry into Jerusalem, the Entombment, the Holy Women.

24. I continue to believe, as was proposed in *L'art religieux du XIIᵉ siècle en France*, 1922, pp. 402 ff., that the tympanum at Cahors antedates the Chartres portals. This opinion has been shared by Mme Lefrançois-Pillion, *Les sculpteurs français du XIIᵉ siècle*, 1937, p. 123 and by M. Rey, *La sculpture romane languedocienne*, 1936, p. 268.
25. The month of January sitting in front of his table is the work of the artist who sculpted the philosophers on the portal of the Virgin ; it could not be by the artist who represented the harvester in July with his very finely woven straw hat, and the great lord of the month of April, with his crown, so delicately chiselled.

**The central portal :
tympanum and voussoirs**

The central portal reveals the heavens. The God of the Day of Judgment appears before man, flanked by the four beasts of the Gospels. This Apocalypse scene had been portrayed with supernatural grandeur by the old sculptor of Moissac. Art became humanised at Chartres. Christ no longer has the terrible countenance of a vision, and his face radiates gentleness rather than majesty. The hand of the master of the statues of the central portal is recognisable in this beautiful Christ figure, and again in the delicate folds in the tunics and the pupils of their eyes actually bored out, enlivening the expression of one of the queens. Surrounding Christ, the sky is peopled with beautiful angels, their upper halves surging from the clouds, and with the Elders of the Apocalypse, sitting on their thrones, carrying a cup in one hand and a musical instrument in the other. Many of these figures, carved in a stone which had no resistance to erosion, are no more than shadows of their former selves. These figures are the work of sculptors of varying talent, but four Elders standing where the voussoirs begin, are outright masterpieces. With the noble figures of kings, their kingdoms are not of this world ; all of them raise their eyes towards the dazzling light of eternity. The detail is exquisite : the crowns, each individual, appear wrought by a goldsmith, the musical instruments assembled by a lute-maker-more perfect work was perhaps never produced in the twelfth century. There is every reason to believe that these fine figures are creations of the sculptor of the magnificent Virgin carrying the Child on the southern portal. Despite the unfortunate erosion, the Lady of Notre-Dame's expression is still visible : she looks up to the sky like the Elders, her crown chiselled equally delicately, the symmetrical folds at the base of her robe similar to those at the base of their tunics[26]. If this attribution is correct, the sculptor of the Virgin, who also carved the Ascension, is the greatest of the twelfth century Chartres school, along with the sculptor of the tall figures on the central portal and the Christ of the Apocalypse.

The apostle figures sitting on the lintel beneath Christ's feet are the work of a skilful craftsman but are lacking all inspiration. The sculptor, apparently trained in the south once again, faithfully repeated the regional hallmark of crossed legs.

**The portail royal :
its capitals and decoration**

The historiated capitals of the columns supporting the three portals form a pleasingly decorative, continuous frieze whose charm lies more in the total effect, however, than in perfection of detail. Their lines have all become indistinct with time and some of them have been deliberately mutilated. They tell the story of the Virgin's parents and of the Virgin herself, according to the Apocryphal Gospels, followed by the Childhood of Christ, together with a few scenes from his public life and his Passion. Errors in the positioning of the capitals when the portal was rebuilt account for some of the iconographical peculiarities and obscure portions of this narrative[27]. Certainly several sculptors worked on these thirty-eight subjects, but they remain rather uniform, with no very apparent differences of style. Certain small figures with prominent eyes recall the statues which were built on the right portal, in the splay positioned to the right of the spectator. Certain scenes betray a southern influence, for example the scene where Christ is arrested in the Garden of Olives — one of the finest works in the series — show traces of the representation of the same episode on a capital of the Daurade cloisters at Toulouse[28] : at the moment of Judas's kiss, one of the soldiers seizes Christ's right arm with savage violence, his raised elbow making a brutal angle, which is repeated at Chartres. The Chartres sculptors also knew Cahors, as the idea of decorating the top of the capitals with architectural motifs in relief comes from there. It is the tympanum at Cahors in fact, which probably offers the oldest example of this : in the Ascension scene, the apostles stand in rows beneath blind arches, crowned by palaces and towers of very delicately designed architecture — motifs borrowed from miniatures. One of the arcades at Cahors frames an apostle who stands

19. Portail Royal, capitals.
Left bay.
The Life of Christ :
Massacre of the Innocents.

26. Another argument must be added. The Virgin of the Saint Anne portal at Notre-Dame in Paris is a copy of the one at Chartres ; here, the Child has several little curls made of separate strands of hair on his forehead, which have been eroded on his counterpart at Chartres. However these curls are exactly the same as the ones we see on the Elders of the Apocalypse at Chartres.
27. The ordering of the scenes is very peculiar. The first part of the narrative begins on the central portal and ends up on the left portal, the second part of the story begins likewise on the same central portal, only to continue on the right portal.
28. Today, in the Musée de Toulouse.

in an extremely unusual position : instead of being seen frontally like the others, he is viewed almost from behind, and a gathered tunic reveals the outlines of his body. A perfectly similar figure may be seen on one of the capitals at Chartres, a parallel which cannot be attributed to chance alone[29]. The evidence becomes more and more striking : the art of the south of France was further developed at Saint-Denis and at Chartres, where it achieved a new perfection.

This series of capitals adds the final touch to a decorated portal of dazzling beauty. Scarcely any smooth columns are to be seen : beneath the statues' feet they become fluted and intricate, between the statues themselves they are carved from top to bottom with miraculous patience. Bending branches and ribbons intertwine, while small figures, centaurs, mermaids, naked women, chimerical birds frolic in the sculptured motifs. This is a goldsmiths' art, and magnificent bases for candelabra could be designed after these columns. The door frames are not left bare, but are decorated with small figures of apostles and prophets with canopies above them. This columnar decoration of the portals and the doorframes was already suggested at Saint-Denis, but such decorative richness married with such refinement was unique to France, and one might add, to Europe as a whole.

Influence of the Chartres portals

These three portals must be imagined as they were when new, at the back of this open air vestibule formed by the projection of the towers, a *hortus conclusus* as it were, adorned with the rarest flowers. These new marvels, suddenly sprung from the soil of France, formed a vision of unknown beauty. The sculptures in all their grandeur were decorated with delicate colours, picked out in gold, whose last traces could still be seen a century ago. The pilgrims stood in wonder on the threshold of the sanctuary, and their understandable reactions account for the immediate attempts to copy these master-pieces.

The Virgin of the Chartres portal, an august image of the cathedral's reigning queen, was reproduced as early as 1164 on the façade of Notre-Dame de Paris, and then on the portals of Bourges cathedral. The lintel representing the Annunciation and the Nativity of this same Chartres portal was copied at La Charité-sur-Loire[30].

It was this central portal, with its tall statues and its Christ in majesty flanked by the four beasts, which was preeminent as a model for other sculptors. Its reputation must have been immense, for a large number of inferior imitations may be found, at Le Mans cathedral, at the cathedrals of Bourges and Angers for example. The abbeys imitated it as well as the episcopal churches : it inspired the portals of Saint-Germain-des-Prés in Paris, Saint-Pourçain in the Bourbonnais district and Nesles-la-Reine in Champagne. Even the Bourgogne area, which had perhaps sent some sculptors to collaborate on the Saint-Denis and Chartres portals, could not resist the masterpiece's influence despite its distinctly original, regional style. The portal at Avallon sought to rival Chartres in magnificence, while other relationships existed between Chartres and the portals of Saint-Bénigne at Dijon and of Saint-Pierre, Nevers, known only from drawings. The South itself, to whom the North was so greatly indebted, welcomed in its turn this art of Royal France : at Toulouse in the Daurade chapter house, the Virgin of Chartres may be found again, looking slightly younger[31]. The façade of Saint-Trophime at Arles, formerly held to be the model of the Chartres portals is but a reinterpretation in the Provençal style.

Many other examples could be added, but all testify to the renown of the beautiful façade. During the second half of the twelfth century, Chartres became the great school of architecture and sculpture in France : its originality and radiant beauty proved irresistible[32].

29. This capital seems to depict Judas asking the priests for the price of his treason. The similarity of the capital at Chartres and the bas-relief at Cahors was recognised by Mme Lefrançois-Pillion, *Les sculpteurs français du XIIe siècle*, p. 122.
30. I do not believe that the portal at La Charité dates before Chartres and provided a model. The artistry at La Charité is more confident and decisive than that at Chartres ; it dates from some twenty years later. There were three shepherds at Chartres, one of which, cut in half when the portal was put back into place has become scarcely visible ; likewise, there are only two shepherds at La Charité.
31. In the Musée de Toulouse.
32. I have devoted a more detailed study to the influence of the Chartres portals in *L'Art religieux du XIIe siècle en France*, ch. XI.

20. Flying buttresses and parapet wells.

21. West façade,
Portail Royal,
central bay.

22. Portail Royal,
central bay.
Figures foretelling
the coming of Christ.

37

23. Portail Royal,
central bay.
Tympanum :
Christ in Glory.

24. Portail Royal,
central bay.
Christ of the tympanum.

38

25. Portail Royal,
central bay.
The Bull of Saint Luke,
with apostles on lintel.

26. Portail Royal.
Pedestal of column figures.

27-28. Portail Royal,
voussoirs.
Elders of the Apocalypse
and angels.

42

Pages 44 and 45 :

29-30. Portail Royal,
central bay.
Column figures.

31. Portail Royal,
central bay.
Column figure.

32. Portail Royal,
central bay.
Column figure, detail.

Pages 48 and 49 :

33. Portail Royal,
left bay.
Ascension.

34. Portail Royal,
right bay.
Virgin portal.

Pages 50 and 51 :

35. Portail Royal.
Ascension portal,
tympanum.

36. Portail Royal.
Virgin portal,
tympanum.

37. Portail Royal,
right bay.
Column figures.

38. Portail Royal,
right bay.
Column figures.

Pages 54 and 55 :

39-40. Portail Royal.
right bay.
Column figures.

41-42. Portail Royal.
right bay.
Column figure.

**43. Portail Royal,
central bay.
Column figure.**

**44. Portail Royal.
Virgin portal,
detail.**

47. Portail Royal.
Tympanum of the Ascension, details.

48. Portail Royal.
Left bay voussoirs.
The works of the months.
The signs of the Zodiac.

Pages 60 and 61 :

45-46. Portail Royal.
Virgin portal,
detail.

49. Angel with sundial.

3. The thirteenth century cathedral

The splendid twelfth century portals so are all the more precious as they were nearly lost when on June 11th, 1194, a terrible fire destroyed Fulbert's old cathedral. Its nave had been covered in timberwork, but the façade was left intact. This façade had been taken down stone by stone a few years previously, as its foundations had been causing some concern. It was moved forward to align with the towers[1], and in all probability, escaped fire damage thanks to this reconstruction, which meant it was even further from the source of the fire, and additionally protected by a vestibule and tribune.

Part of the town was destroyed at the same time as the cathedral, but the townsfolk, forgetting their distress, had but one thought, for the reliquary casket of Notre-Dame. For three days, they were unable to approach the smoking ruins, and with much anguish wondered whether the Holy Tunic had been destroyed in the flames, as well as the sanctuary. On the third day, some clerks were seen leaving the crypt where

1. The excavations carried out by Lefèvre-Pontalis in 1901 and 1903 proved that the foundations were insufficent, and that the façade had moved a little. The reconstruction led to some mistakes in the disposition of the statues, and as the left and right portals were narrowed even further, two of the figures had to be cut in half. See *Congrès archéol. Chartres*, 1901 and *Mém. de la Soc. archéol.* d'Eure-et-Loir, vol. XIII.

they had taken refuge, carrying the reliquary on their shoulders. The public celebrated with great joy : the holy relic was saved ; nothing had been lost.

The bishop, the canons and the townsfolk decided at once to build a new church, more magnificent than its predecessor, and offered part of their own fortunes as a contribution to the project. The fervour in the town reached the countryside, and suddenly the spirit of faith which fifty years previously had roused the peasants of the Beauce region and neighbouring areas was reborn. The *Livre des Miracles de Notre-Dame* written in Latin and translated into French verse by Jean Le Marchant recounts this second epic[2]. The multitudes gathered, as once before, loaded the heavy carts with stones, wheat, wine and all that the labourers might find useful, and dragged the burdens to Chartres. The townsfolk of Pithiviers, their necks in harness, became so exhausted travelling through the Beauce region, that those from Puiset wanted to take their place. The offer was refused, however, as the former were reluctant to lose any rewards of their pilgrimage. France still subscribed the principles of heroism, and the desire to prove individual worth through sacrifice, which had led the crusaders to the Orient, was in other forms as powerful as ever.

The fire which burnt down Notre-Dame, the Virgin's most famous church, affected the whole of northern France. Alms collectors went from town to town carrying reliquaries and calling upon the local congregations to be generous. Men wept when they heard the tale of disaster, and no one refused Notre-Dame de Chartres an offering. The *Livre des Miracles* tells us how, in the church at Soissons, a young Englishman, deeply moved along with the rest, resolved to make a gift to the Virgin. He had a golden necklace which he had bought for a girl in London whom he loved. A battle raged in his heart but he conquered his initial misgivings and the love of heaven triumphed over the love of earthly things : he contributed the necklace. The following night, three women of the rarest beauty appeared in a vision ; the most beautiful turned to him and declared she was Notre-Dame herself. Having thanked him for his sacrifice, she showed him that she was wearing the golden necklace around her throat. Richard the Lionheart heard this story, and was so touched that when the alms collectors came to England, he was not content simply to offer them his donation, but wanted to carry the reliquary casket on his own shoulders. At the time, the English king was at war with Philippe-Auguste, but the influence of Notre-Dame de Chartres reconciled the two enemies.

New miracles thus proclaimed the renaissance of the cathedral. The enthusiasm and love that went into the building are immediately apparent : historical studies confirm this first impression.

The new cathedral

Chartres cathedral radiates the genius of two great centuries : the western façade demonstrates French Romanesque sculpture at its height of perfection and influence, while the thirteenth century Gothic style was born and flowered in this incomparable architectural masterpiece. Without Chartres, neither Reims, Amiens or Beauvais could be understood as cathedrals.

The thirteenth century architect was anonymous : if his name was inscribed according to contemporary custom within the maze drawn on the paving stones it has long disappeared.

Few cathedrals were built so rapidly as Chartres. Begun in 1194, the vaults and arches were completed by 1220. The work began with the nave whose flying buttresses date stylistically from before those of the apse. It was important to build quickly for the sake of the pilgrims who held their services in Fulbert's vast crypt while the building programme was in hand. A provisional choir stall, made of light materials, was apparently quickly erected to allow them to worship the holy reliquary.

Trained on the twelfth century cathedral sites, the chief architect had various options open to him. No two cathedrals were similar : the twelfth century had not ceased building great churches and never had there been so much stylistic variety. Laon had simple side aisles ; Paris had double side aisles ; Sens had no transept ; Noyon had a transept with two semicircular apses at either end, while the apses were rectangular at Laon ; Senlis had an ambulatory with radiating chapels, Paris had an ambulatory

---

2. *Le Livre des Miracles de Notre-Dame* by Jean Le Marchant was published by G. Duplessis in 1855 ; the original Latin version was rediscovered by Antoine Thomas in the Vatican Library in 1881 and published the same year in the *Biblioth. de l'École des Chartres.*

without chapels. However, there were various common features : all had sexpartite vaults, which lead to the alternation of strong and weak pillars in the nave, a feature that was sometimes disguised. All except Sens had galleries.

With an admirable daring, the chief architect of Chartres broke with his past, and resolutely embarked on a forward looking project. First he abandoned the sexpartite vault based on a square ground plan, and replaced it with a vault which had a simple intersection of ogival cross ribs on a barlong plan, an innovation sanctioned by all the great thirteenth century cathedrals. Then he did away with the galleries, a decision all the more courageous in that he saw two magnificent churches with galleries completed at that time : Laon cathedral and Notre-Dame de Paris. The suppression of the galleries transformed the whole church interior at a stroke, changing both the proportions and the lighting. The example was widely followed. These innovations, however, deserve more detailed study.

The plan and elevation

When the plan of Chartres was drawn up, the architect faced certain constraints. The underground church determined the length and breadth of the church above, as to fill in the venerated crypt and build the new church in its place was out of the question. The crypt walls, reinforced, served as foundations for the new church. Free, however, to design the transept, the architect gave it dimensions so broad it became a veritable transverse nave with side aisles, a feature which would be copied at Reims and Amiens.

The most ingenious solutions were employed to build the ambulatory with its radiating chapels upon the Carolingian ambulatory and Fulbert's subterranean chapels. The irregularities which are noticeable in the arrangement of the columns and the unequal depth of the chapels were elements imposed on him by the foundations[3]. He was able to overcome all the obstacles, and give the ambulatory something of the lightness of the one at Saint-Denis. Nevertheless, alterations were necessary when the Chartres' ambulatory served as a model for the cathedrals at Reims and Amiens.

Chartres' chief architect shows his greatest originality, however, in the elevation design rather than in the plan. The raised gallery was replaced by a simple triforium which provides ornament for the bare walls and an idea of monumental scale, for the small columns, each the height of a man, give a sense of the elevation of the vault. The abolition of the galleries had two consequences : the nave windows could be enlarged, and the side aisles could be raised in height. Much lighter in appearance, the side aisles let more light through their windows into the nave. The gallery was abolished above all, however, for the sake of the upper storey windows. The cathedrals at Laon and Paris for example, completed towards the end of the twelfth century, had the very simplest of windows in the nave ; their dimensions strictly limited by the presence of a gallery, with a triforium above it at Laon, and a series of rose windows at Paris. There was also concern that the wall might be weakened if the openings in it were too large. The chief architect at Chartres, more familiar with the potentials of the new architecture, was the first with the courage to open up the whole bay and do away with the wall almost completely. Instead of a simple window, he pierced a double window and reunited the two openings with a mullion, an enduring feature of Gothic architecture, though on this occasion the mullion remains a division built up with a vertical row of bricks and is not yet the typical small column rising from a single base. A rose window of magnificent proportions and unparalleled beauty was placed above the double window, as part of the ensemble. The upper regions of the wall, now opened to the light, poured illumination into the nave. The thirteenth century window had been invented : its surface would increase at Reims and Amiens and become disproportionately large at Beauvais. The beginnings of this aspiration towards light, so characteristic of Gothic architecture is first seen at Chartres, where the chief architect first understood that the junction of the diagonal ribs and the flying buttress, cancelling the thrust of the vaults, rendered the wall practically useless.

Not only the windows, but the pillars of the nave assumed new forms. The powerful monocylindrical column at Laon and Paris disappeared and was replaced by a more complex support. Each architectural mass was divided up into four columns : three of them bore the weight of the arcades of the nave and the transverse ribs of the

52. Nave vault.

3. This was demonstrated by Albert Mayeux in the *Mém. de la Soc. archéol. d'Eure-et-Loir,* vol. XIII, p. 49.

53. North portal.
African
beneath the feet
of the Queen of Sheba.

side aisles ; the fourth, turned towards the nave, was joined from the capital upwards, by four small columns rising towards the vault and corresponding with its ribs : transverse ribs, diagonal ribs and wall arches. These multiple pillars would become standard for thirteenth century cathedrals[4]. There is every reason to believe that the Chartres architect was the first to use this formation, as the nave at Notre-Dame in Paris does not appear to be a precedent.

In Paris the divided pillar with four columns is seen only in the last bay of the nave, preceding the massive pier supporting the towers. This part of Notre-Dame de Paris dates from 1210 at the earliest[5]. At Chartres, from as early as 1194, the master architect had drawn up his plan, and by 1210 the nave must have been vaulted, because the vaults of the entire church had been built by 1220. It may thus be deduced that the idea came from Chartres. At Chartres, the five small columns that rise towards the vault are twice cut by the band of the triforium and the line of windows, marking the

4. At Chartres, there is a curious alternation in design : a cylindrical pillar divided into four octagonal columns alternates with an octagonal pillar divided into four cylindrical columns. This is a final reminiscence of the alternating pattern of pillars that was so frequent in the twelfth century.
5. This is the very likely date given by M. Marcel Aubert in *Notre-Dame de Paris ; sa place dans l'histoire de l'architecture*, 1920, p. 47.

**54. North portal.
Marcoul
beneath the feet
of Solomon.**

division into storeys with broad horizontal lines[6]. Reims and Amiens remained faithful to the architectural conception at Chartres, with the clarity of its divisions ; but at Beauvais, the desire for height predominated, and the architect designed small columns which rose in one flight up to the beginnings of the vault. A new age was declared which would be dominated by uninterrupted vertical lines.

. The nave at Chartres thus had a completely new appearance, thanks to the simplicity of the vaults, the size of its windows and the form of its pillars ; and these new ideas were soon imitated. There is also the desire to elevate matter : a spiritual phenomenon, although it can be measured in building terms. The vaults et Noyon and those at Senlis are 22 metres high, those at Laon 24 metres high, at Paris 35 metres high, and at Chartres 37 metres high ; shortly those at Reims were to be suspended from a height of 38 metres, from Amiens 42 metres, from Beauvais 48 metres. Experience, calculations, the use of set-square and compasses do not explain it all : the imaginative elements of poetry and spiritual aspiration remain, essential but intangible.

Pages 72 and 73 :
55. Chartres cathedral
viewed from the south.

6. At Chartres, the small columns applied to the four pillars of the central square of the transept rise by themselves without interruption from the paving stones up to the vault.

The architect at Chartres dreamed perhaps of raising his
was forestalled by the unaccustomed breadth of the nave,
foundations of the crypt. Fulbert's old nave, covered with a s
reached a width of 16.4 metres without any trouble. This d
new nave at Chartres, much wider than that of all other Fre
Noyon for example, is only 8.5 metres wide, at Laon 1
12 metres wide and at Reims and Amiens, 14.6 metres wi
courage on the part of the architect to envisage, in 1194
metres wide, suspended from a height of 37 metres. If
problem tackled by any cathedral builder to date.

The remaining problem was to resist the thrust
complicated by the fact that the architect had done awa
galleries, often with a buttress wall above them and hidde
maintain the equilibrium of the whole. The elements
originally thought to have appeared at the same time, ar
supposed to be contemporary with the diagonal ribs ; tod
buttress appeared later, and that the oldest Gothic churc
buttresses alone, by galleries or by little walls concealed under the roof. The first flying
buttresses were applied as an emergency measure against the apses or naves which
threatened to collapse as they had very little resistance to the thrust of the vaults[7].

The apse of Notre-Dame de Paris did not have flying buttresses originally. However,
the architect who built the nave included them in his design around 1180. He was
perhaps the first to understand that the vault of diagonal ribs should henceforth be
inseparable from the flying buttresses. The architect at Chartres took the architecture
of Notre-Dame in Paris as a model when he supported his powerful vaults by flying
buttresses planned from the initial stage[8]. However, he understood that the thrust of
the vault was diffused, and was not concentrated merely on the spot where the
transverse ribs and the diagonal ribs met, but over a much larger spread. Moreover a
single flying buttress did not seem sufficient to him : above the first he raised a second,
and his inventive genius led to another original idea, imitated so many times after him :
he joined them into one unit by means of small columns. Nothing more robust than this
fragment of a wheel with its spokes formed by stocky columns can be imagined. This
double flying buttress was positioned against a simple projecting buttress whose
strength defies the centuries. The rude stone from Berchères, with its rugged surface
complements this force. The work possesses a heroic grandeur. Nowhere is the genius
and the confidence of Chartres' chief architect revealed to more advantage than in
these buttresses, the flying buttresses and the cyclopeian blocks of the foundations.
The only ornaments selected for each of these powerful projections were two rosettes
and a statue of a bishop in a niche.

In 1316, after a visit from three Parisian experts including Pierre de Chelles, the
master builder of Notre-Dame, it was decided that an extra flying buttress should be
constructed at Chartres, to be positioned against the uppermost part of the wall.
Perhaps this showed an excess of precaution, but unfortunately the work of the
original architect lost something of its beauty[9].

On the apse, a difficulty was encountered, since the choir was surrounded by a
double side aisle and radiating chapels. Had the flying buttress been just one extended
span, it would have been inordinately long. The architect at Notre-Dame in Paris who
built its nave with double side aisles provided the solution for Chartres. In Paris, the
flying buttress was divided into two parts by means of an intermediate buttress — an
elegant solution, which in Paris has disappeared through restoration, but which still
exists at Chartres. These new flying buttresses do not have the overwhelming power of
the originals, and their design, which is less robust, demonstrates that the apse was
built after the nave.

56. North side :
buttresses and flying buttresses.

7. This happened with the apse of Saint-Germain-des-Prés. See Lefevre-Pontalis, *L'origine des arcs-boutants. Congrès archéol.*, held in Paris, in 1919.
8. With an excess of precaution, the master architect at Chartres built a buttress wall above the side aisles.
9. V. Mortet, *L'expertise de la cathédrale de Chartres en 1316*, in the *Congrès archéol. de Chartres*, 1900, p. 308.

57. Apse : view from the north east.

58. Apse and north tower
of apse.

The transept façades.
The rose windows,
the towers

Chartres' great architect clearly did not invent everything, and when the occasion presented itself, he did not hesitate to borrow outstanding ideas from the work of his predecessors. He probably spent his apprenticeship on the busy cathedral projects at Noyon, Senlis, Paris and Laon. Certainly Laon cathedral must have left a very strong impression on him. No artist could remain unmoved by this wonderful church. Few monuments in the Middle Ages contain so much poetry as this great cathedral rising with its five towers from the summit of its citadel. Here, in all its majesty, we see the century of the crusaders and the troubadours. Laon's role in relation to cathedral architecture of the time was very important. Architects came from far and wide in search of inspiration. In Germany, parts of the cathedral were imitated at Bamberg, Naumburg, Halberstadt, Magdeburg and Limbourg-on-Lahn ; in France, the architect of Reims cathedral used it as inspiration for his façade and his towers, the architect at Amiens did likewise for his porch, and the architect at Lisieux for his nave.

Chartres' architectural debt to Laon cathedral may be seen in the two façades framed by the towers of the transept. Laon offered the finest model for the façade of the northern transept. Above the doors a huge rose window was placed above a row of five lancets and was itself dominated by a huge gallery. Throughout the thirteenth century, this felicitous idea can always be recognised despite any ornamentation. These broad outlines were respected by the architect at Chartres, but he added his own original touches. The rose window at Laon was delightful : it consisted of a central rose surrounded by a coronet of eight smaller roses, but the Chartres architect, judging that the interstices took up too much space in the design made his rose window more ethereal by making a lighter setting for the panes of stained glass[10]. In addition, he wanted the five accompanying lancets to be enlarged to make one luminous unit along with the rose window, again creating more emphasis on the stained glass itself. The total effect, lightened in this way, was so beautiful that the thirteenth century façades of Saint-Denis, of Notre-Dame de Paris and all their derivatives simply amplified and enriched the one at Chartres.

It was not only the façades of the transept that the Chartres architect borrowed from Laon, but in addition the two towers that framed them with this design[11] ; the façades of the transept are related to the principal façade and seem, in fact, to reproduce it. As broad as the nave, the transept at Chartres terminates in a similar way at either end, with a façade between two towers. The two steeples of the western façade should therefore have been accompanied by the four towers of the transept. Surprisingly enough, the Chartres architect believed he should add two more to these six towers. He copied the two steeples built at the beginning of the apse he had seen at Noyon, following a tradition which dates back to Carolingian times. Chartres cathedral should therefore, have had eight towers, and judging by the strength of the pillars of the square of the transept, perhaps nine[12]. Laon had just seven, but only five had been raised above the height of the roof, and these five towers give it a grandeur which is unique. It is hard to imagine what Chartres would have been like if its eight towers had been completed : in fact all but those of the main façade stop at the line of the roof. The architects at Reims and later those at Rouen had the same idea and were no more successful in realising it. The architects of these churches dedicated to Notre-Dame wanted them to be like those canopies with several towers sculpted above the Virgin's head, but is was soon realised that this dream was impossibly ambitious.

The art of the Middle Ages, born of Christianity, contains within it a sense of the illimitable. One has but to compare these churches with five, seven and eight steeples to the basilicas of Rome, which had no exterior projections, and had no campaniles for a long period, to realise the vast difference between Gothic aspirations and the art of proportion, born of classical genius. Vast sums would have had to be found to build two great porches on the north and south faces, to cover them with statues and to fill the windows and rose windows with stained glass. Thus not one of these towers was

59. South side : buttresses.

10. On the west façade at Chartres, he made a rose window that bears much more resemblance to the one at Laon. Villard de Honnecourt admired it and drew it in his sketchbook when he came to Chartres.

11. The master architect at Laon was himself bearing in mind the two towers of Notre-Dame de Tournai, each of which frame the apses which terminate the arms of the transept ; but by replacing the two apses with two façades, he created an organic whole. See E. Lambert, *Gazette des Beaux-Arts*, 1926, vol. XIII, p. 321.

12. A small tower was built above the centre of the transept in the fourteenth century ; a more magnificent one had doubtless been intended.

60. Flying buttresses at transept crossing.

61. South side : flying buttresses, detail.

completed at Chartres for the priority was to protect the vaults with a huge timber-work frame, and the frame itself by a roofing of lead as quickly as possible. This framework, admired for seven centuries, was called "the forest", because a whole forest had been needed to build it, and the long alleys of forest trees could be seen reconstructed there. It burnt down in 1836, a disaster which moved the whole of France. Nothing remained of the "forest", and the fifteen hundred slabs of lead which used to cover it were transformed into molten streams. An iron framework replaced this thirteenth century masterpiece, and a copper covering replaced the slabs of lead.

In 1224, the bulk of the construction work was finished and the decoration of the cathedral well advanced. The three portals created at each of the entrances of the transept had received their tympana, their tall statues and the voussoir statuettes ; nearly all the windows were filled with their stained glass. No cathedral had ever been built in so short a space of time, and never had masons, sculptors and glaziers worked with such enthusiasm. The work was approaching completion and promised to be magnificent. It was thought that the cathedral could be even more impressive, that its attractions could be increased with more ornament, that additional statues would make it more instructive, that more great and moving thoughts could be expressed in stone. The decision was therefore taken to build at each of the ends of the transept, in front of the three great portals, a monumental porch, to be decorated with new figures and new stories. It is not certain whether the architect who planned such elaborate annexes was the same one who gave the overall design such noble and simple proportions.

Once more, it was Laon cathedral which provided the inspiration. A porch with three entrances jutted out from its façade, and thrust the three portals back into the half light. Dark and shadowy at certain hours of the day, this porch in all its austerity accentuates still further the grave, solemn aspect of Laon cathedral. The three entrances of the porch extend down to the portals as three galleries, separated by solid walls[13]. The entire decor consists of gables above the three entrance arcades, with pinnacles rising between them. At Chartres, the porch at Laon reappears transfigured, however, by an architectural stroke of genius, for the solid gallery walls have disappeared, everything is open, all is light. The parallel vaults stop at the lintels, allowing for a free passage in front of the portals. The three entrance arcades no longer rest on solid masonry, but on pilasters decorated with bas-reliefs, or on columns which have simple projections bearing statues, with empty spaces left between them. Bands of statuettes decorate the vaults and form the voussoirs of the arcades. Vine-leaf scrolls surround the columns, while branches of oak decorate their bases. These porches, in conjunction with the portals, form a most splendid whole, and are so closely united that they seem to spring from the same creative thought. The southern porch has a heavier type of architecture and less richness of detail than the northern one, and is older in all probability. It must have been started as early as 1224, at the moment when the canons ordered the traders who had set up stalls in front of the southern portal, to take their goods elsewhere[14]. The northern porch was started a little later, and the architect added some excellent improvements and some more decoration to his work. He multiplied the entrances, creating a lighter effect, and enriched it with ornamental statues on pedestals of the most refined design. It is not known why he did not completely finish the upper parts. Unlike the southern porch these were not crowned with the four pinnacles adorned with statues — another reference to Laon cathedral.

These two porches, which must be imagined painted and gilded like the portals, doubtless aroused an intense admiration, but no cathedral architect ever dared reproduce their magnificence. A feeble version may be found at Léon cathedral in Spain. The architect who completed the upper parts of the façade at Vézelay had this fine model in mind : the five arcades of unequal height which he pierced on the first storey above the space of the porch derive from Chartres. If the central arcade were to be enlarged, the design of the northern porch at Chartres would be revealed. Statues whose style is close to those at Chartres may also be seen at Vézelay.

13. It seems there had originally been a means of communication between the three galleries which was shut off at quite an early stage.
14. René Merlet, *La cath. de Chartres*, p. 56 and *Cartul. de N.-D. de Chartres*, vol. II p. 103.

64. Transept wall.

66. Vault at the crossing.

65. Transept pillar and choir.

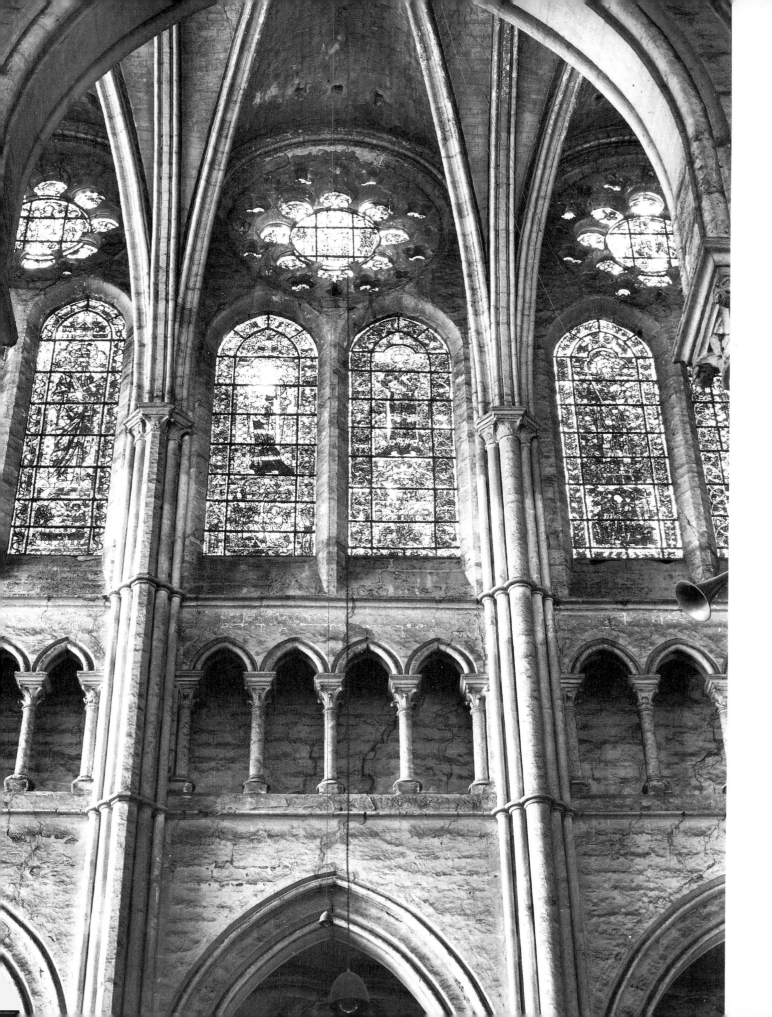

67. Wall of nave.

68. Transept and south rose window.

70. Nave, detail.

71. Vaulting ribs.

72. Crossing seen
from triforium.

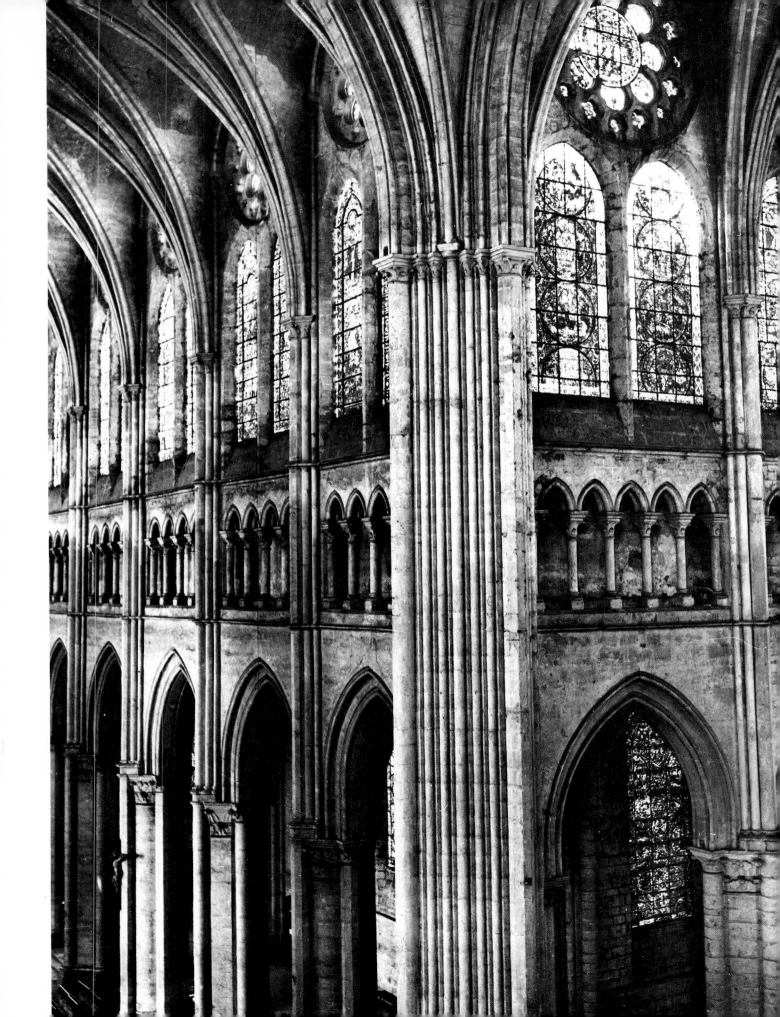

Pages 94 and 95 :

73. South side aisle.

74. Ambulatory.

75. Triforium.

76. North portal, central bay.
Socle figures
beneath the feet of the prophets.

4. Overall view : the sculpture

The innumerable statues and statuettes of the portals and porches create a world whose meanings can be explored more fully by focusing on the development in the conception and design of the whole. The plan was simple at first, but later became more complicated and extensive. Originally the architect had planned only a single portal at each end of the transept[1]. The northern portal was to have copied the portal at Senlis, completed a few years previously, and which represented two subjects : firstly the Triumph of the Virgin, seated in the heavens, with a crown on her head, to the right of her Son, and secondly the Annunciation of the Saviour by Old Testament prophets. The south portal should also have had two subjects : on the tympanum and the voussoirs one was to see the Last Judgment, an imposing subject, created in Languedoc, but which was now known in royal France thanks to the portals at Saint-Denis and at Corbeil. In the embrasures, tall statues of the apostles lined up on either side of Christ the teacher, would recall the propagation of the Gospel throughout the world, and the spread of the divine Word, according to which men should be judged.

These two portals were already taking shape in the workshop, when the architect decided to create two more portals in each arm of the transept. This was doubtless on the orders of the bishop and chapter who wished to treat the great themes more extensively than could be managed in two portals alone.

---

1. Each portal was to have been accompanied by two windows, whose traces may be seen on the arm of the north transept.

At the south end of the transept, the two new portals told the story of the conquest of the world by the divine Word. The one on the right, which shows Christ as teacher and judge, is dedicated to the martyrs whose blood was the seed of the new religion. The one on the left of the Saviour celebrates the Confessors : fathers of the Church, bishops, missionaries of the faith, who demonstrated the virtue of the Gospels to mankind through books, words, or their own examples. This history of the progress of faith and charity was the only one which merited the telling, for these grave and learned thirteenth century theologians.

Indifferent to material progress, the Middle Ages never dreamed of working except in the realms of the spirit. When a porch was built in front of these portals, towards 1224, two of its pillars[2] were decorated with little scenes, where new episodes in the histories of martyrs and confessors could be read. Two other pillars, those in the centre, represented the opposition of the Virtues and the Vices, images which lead the mind back to the Last Judgment on the central portal, where vice and virtue are weighed in the archangel's scales. The twenty-four Elders of the Apocalypse are there too, and complete the depiction of the Last Judgment. The façade as a whole thus develops the same idea ; it speaks in a language of great clarity and seems to say to the spectator : "Christ, and after him the propagators of the Gospel, apostles, martyrs and confessors, have revealed to mankind the path which leads to Salvation. May they follow it, and on the Last Day they shall merit a place on the right hand of the Judge".

Two portals were also created on the north arm of the transept after those of the south. The central portal, as was mentioned, represented the Triumph of the Virgin and the Annunciation of the Messiah by the patriarchs and prophets — ideas which were easy to bring together as the Virgin and the Messiah were inseparable. A new portal (the one which is on the left) was dedicated to the Virgin. At Chartres it was believed that Notre-Dame could never be adequately praised and celebrated. On the old west front, it is true, the pilgrims could see the Annunciation, the Visitation, the Nativity and the Adoration of the Magi twice over, but the small figures on the lintel and the even smaller figures on the capitals were not enough for their piety. On this new portal, magnificent statues showed the Annunciation, and the Visitation, with an unprecedented nobility. As for the Nativity, the Adoration of the Shepherds and the Adoration of the Magi, they took up the whole tympanum. The voussoirs also celebrated the Virgin's perfections with subtle analogies : here one could see the parable of the Wise Virgin's triumph over the Foolish Virgins, the triumph of the Virtues over the Vices, and finally, twelve unexplained female figures which are perhaps the twelve fruits of the spirit which Saint Paul speaks of, twelve virtues adorning the Virgin's soul.

This richly decorated portal has its counterpart on the other side of the central portal, with a sombre portal, as full of gravity and pathos as the Old Testament itself. It completes the central portal : to the solemn figures of patriarchs and prophets which form its decor, new figures are added who also announce the Incarnation through symbols. Thus Baalam, Solomon, and the Queen of Sheba, Joseph and Judith in the embrasures, the trials of Job on the tympanum and on the voussoirs, episodes in the story of Samson, Gideon, Esther and Judith, are depicted sometimes prefiguring the Saviour himself, sometimes the Virgin. These characters, would be joined a little later by still others on the porch.

The whole of this north façade, then, represents the Old Testament and the Virgin, the supreme flower of the World before Christ. This symbolism conforms perfectly to medieval tradition : the North, the realm where light is paler and the sun burns less fiercely, is that which befits the Old Testament, according to theological tradition ; the South, where light and heat shine forth, is the realm of the Gospels. And likewise, as we have seen, the south façade is dedicated, for the most part, to the spread of the Gospels[3]. Such is the theological structure which governs the two imposing façades of Chartres cathedral. New resonances will appear when the architectural details are closely studied.

77-78. South porch pillar, Confessors' bay. Martyrs' bay.

2. They are the ones on the far right and left of the porch.
3. The Last Judgment should have been depicted on the western façade ; for the Middle Ages, the West, realm of the evening, realm of the setting sun, is the realm of the last evening of the world. But the western façade already has its three magnificent portals, under the aegis of Christ, the Judge of the Apocalypse.

It seems logical to study the portals at Chartres in the order in which they were created, an order which can be confidently restored. Following it one can trace the development of sculpture during the first half of the thirteenth century.

The northern façade.
The triumph
of the Virgin portal

No doubt, at Chartres, as at other cathedrals, Notre-Dame in Paris, Laon and Bourges, the designers did not wait for the completion of the structure before planning the decoration. As soon as the architect had removed the remains of the old cathedral and constructed the foundations of the new one, as soon as he had drawn up his plans, the sculptors started work. One may confidently suppose that they were already starting work on the tympanum, the voussoirs and the statues for the Triumph of the Virgin portal by 1197. At that time both the clergy and the artist were filled with admiration for the portal at Senlis which was to serve as an important model. It was being copied at that moment at Mantes, and was to be copied later at Laon. For the first time on a cathedral façade, at Senlis, the genealogical tree of the Virgin had been portrayed together with the scene of her death, surrounded by the apostles, the resurrection of her body, raised from the tomb by angels and finally her triumph in the heavens. For the first time also, the statues of the patriarchs and prophets had been seen, ranged according to their centuries, and announcing the coming of Jesus Christ with a sign or symbol. Here, artistic traditions were rediscovered that reach back to the art at Saint-Denis[4] and the thinking of Suger, for the Triumph of the Virgin, the Tree of Jesse and the figures symbolising Christ dated back to him. The portal at Senlis must have been completed around 1185, because in 1189 it was already being copied in Piedmont at the Church of Vezzolano[5]. Thus it was already twelve years old when it became a model for the sculptors at Chartres. The Chartres portal is conceived with a greater breadth of design than the Senlis model, and it is nearly always superior to the original. The scene of the Triumph of the Virgin is ordered in a more harmonious way and with a greater delicacy of feeling : seated on the right hand of Jesus, Mary is no longer rigidly upright, but gently inclines her crowned head before her Son with a touching modesty. Christ is nobler, seated with more majesty ; his gathered draperies are pleated with an almost classical elegance. In the voussoirs the Virgin's ancestors are (more aptly) framed by the branches of the Tree of Jesse. On the lintel, however, the artist at Senlis has the advantage. The Resurrection of the Virgin is one of the masterpieces of the twelfth century ; the angels, light as swallows, lift the body of the Mother of their God from its sepulchre with spirit, and with a passionate ardour that contains more love than respect. The balance and the symmetry of the group at Chartres should be greatly appreciated but when compared with the original design at Senlis, it must be conceded that for once, reason has held sway over inspiration.

The statues of patriarchs and prophets on the Senlis portal were restored during the last century ; all the heads were remade, together with many of the attributes. Fortunately, however, the casts at the Musée des Monuments français in Paris, which were taken prior to the restoration allow us to see them in their former state. Examination proves that the sculptors at Chartres copied the statues of the Senlis portal, just as they had imitated the tympanum and the voussoirs. But at Chartres the conception was grander and the art itself became ennobled, judging by the mutilated heads of two of these statues at Senlis which have recently been rediscovered[6].

These ten figures at Chartres have a profound meaning. They are arranged in chronological order, and at the same time as they announce the coming of Christ, they recount the history of the world. They confirm the great divisions adopted by the scholars and theologians of the Middle Ages : Melchizedeck, Abraham and Isaac, correspond to the period of humanity when mankind lived under the law of circumcision. Moses, Samuel and David represent the generations which lived under written laws and worshipped God in the temple. Isaiah and Jeremiah, Simeon the Elder, and Saint John the Baptist express the period of the days of prophecy, which continued until the coming of Jesus Christ. Saint Peter comes last : wearing a dalmatic robe, and crowned with a diadem, and bearing the keys and the chalice[7], he announces the reign

**79. South portal voussoir.
Last Judgment, detail.**

4. A few figures still have crossed legs.
5. The sculptures at Vezzolano do not take up a whole semi-circular portal, but are figured on a rood-screen in two rows. As at Senlis, we see the death of the Virgin, her body raised from the tomb by angels, her triumph in the heavens beside her son and finally the figures on the Tree of Jesse. The quality of the work is much lower than at Senlis, but the imitation is obvious. I have demonstrated the parallels in a book entitled : *Rome et ses vieilles églises*, Paris, Flammarion, 1942, p. 214.
6. *Bulletin monum.* 1938, article by M. Aubert.
7. Only the foot of the chalice remains.

80. South portal,
Martyrs' bay.
Saint Theodore.

81. South portal,
Martyrs' bay.
Saint George.

of the Church and the last age of the world. Each of these great figures presents a symbol which prefigures Christ : Melchizedeck bears the chalice, Abraham lays his hand on Isaac's head, Moses grasps the bronze serpent, Samuel holds the sacrificial lamb, David the crown of thorns, Isaiah the Rod of Jesse, Jeremiah the cross, Simeon the Divine Child, Saint John the Baptist the lamb, and finally Saint Peter the chalice. The mysterious chalice which appears at the start of the sequence in the hands of Melchizedeck, is found again in those of Saint Peter, a felicitous idea, which was not expressed at Senlis, where neither Melchizedeck or Saint Peter can be seen. Thus we come full circle. The Old Testament appears to us here as it was for the Middle Ages : a series of prefigurations of Christ of which the meaning becomes increasingly clear.

These extraordinary statues fittingly express the lofty ideas they represent. They remain closely linked to the architecture and are governed by a rigid immobility : their arms are stuck to their bodies, their attributes clasped to their chests. For half a century the aesthetic of the column figure was hardly modified ; there were merely a few heads which started to move out of alignment with the body, bending forwards or turning slightly. The faces, however, were of a singular grandeur, evoking a race of men no longer on this earth. These figures are grave, as befits the harbingers of God's word, and also sad, as those who prophesy events which they will not see. A few of them are unforgettable : the Melchizedeck at Chartres with his pontifical diadem, his long flowing beard and his distant look, equals the mysterious Melchizedeck of the Bible in his majesty. Moses, with his long face, full of nobility and gentleness, has his eyes fixed on the future. Samuel, with the sacrificial veil on his head, and a pensive expression, offers the lamb in sacrifice, dreaming of another victim. As for Saint John the Baptist, with his wild appearance, his brow furrowed with wrinkles, and the long locks of his untamed beard, he is one of the most imposing figures of the Precursor ever conceived in the history of art. Here then, is how these modest carvers of stone, imagined for themselves these Old Testament heroes. Posterity may have overlooked their names, but their instructive feeling for grandeur and their imaginitive response to the scriptures are triumphantly revealed.

In 1204, the Count of Blois sent the head of Saint Anne from Constantinople to Chartres. "The head of the mother, says the *Cartulaire,* was received with great joy in the daughter's church"[8]. It was at that time, no doubt, that the statue of Saint Anne carrying the Virgin as a child was sculpted. It stands against the pier as the finishing touch for the Triumph of the Virgin portal, which must have been installed by 1205.

This art at Chartres is grave, austere, ecclesiastical in character ; but from time to time, the world of nature is glimpsed in all its candour and gentleness. Beneath the feet of each of the prophetic statues, there is a gracefully twisted column. At its base and at the top it is adorned with a few clover leaves, a twig of beech or of wild roses, a vine shoot. Spring — a timid spring — begins to appear. It blossoms a little more freely above the heads of the prophets of the Old Testament, on the capitals which crown them. A profound change is felt : a transformation of the decorative arts. The monsters who came from Asia, filling the Romanesque churches with their strange presence, their occasional wild grandeur, vanish ; the flowers of field and forest take their place, and bedeck the Gothic church with a new grace. The façades at Saint-Denis, Senlis and Mantes have as yet shown us nothing like this. These twisted columns decked with leafy garlands and these capitals mantled in foliage reappear on the six portals at Chartres ; it is the start of a flowering which will be one of the beauties of Reims cathedral.

**The southern façade.
The triumph
of the Virgin portal**

The statues of the prophets of the Triumph of the Virgin portal had just been completed when the statues of the apostles on the southern façade, which represents the Last Judgment, were begun. It was natural to associate the apostles with the Last Judgment as, according to the Gospel, they were to be the Judge's assessors on the Last Day[9]. At Beaulieu, at Saint-Denis and at Laon, the apostles are seated near Christ, separating the good from the evil, but at Chartres a new idea was added to the old ; the apostles have their Master in their midst. He is teaching them his word, the word they

8. *Cartul. de N.-D. de Chartres,* vol. III, p. 89 and p. 178 ; and Riant, *Exuviae Constantinop.,* vol. I, p. 73.
9. Matthew, XIX, 28.

shall make know to the world, and by which the world shall be judged. There is no difficulty in recognising the parallels between these statues of apostles and those of the patriarchs on the northern porch ; again the arms are stuck to their sides, the attributes clasped to their chests, again the long faces are seen, with the flowing beards which end with a small curl. Even the pedestals are designed in the same manner. The patriarchs and the prophets have small figures beneath their feet, some of which are relevant to their mission. Abraham has the ram which was substituted for Isaac, Isaiah has Jesse, from whose side springs the genealogical tree of Christ, Saint Peter has the symbolic stone of the Church. The apostles rest their feet on the tyrants who put them to death, and over whom, today, they triumph. This is the origin of a tradition which would continue throughout the Middle Ages : that of the martyrs trampling on their executioners. Chartres was the first of the great Gothic cathedrals to show such a series of apostles. In their hands they bear some instruments of their torture which are now the insignia of victory. Saint Peter and Saint Andrew have the cross, Saint James the Less the fuller's yard, Saint Bartholomew the knife, Saint Paul the sword, Saint James the Great has another sword, but he already carries the bread hamper and the scallop shells of Saint James of Compostella. At this date, the attributes of the other apostles had not yet been determined.

Compared with the patriarchs and the prophets of the northern portals, certain apostles seem to bear them a very great resemblance. Isaiah hardly differs from Saint Simon, and Saint Matthew seems to be a copy of the prophet Elijah[10]. Sometimes the same hand can be recognised, and it would not be inaccurate to date the execution of the apostle statues at the very beginning of the thirteenth century.

It must be recognised, nevertheless, that these two series of statues did not arouse the same sentiments. The sadness which weighs on the countenances of the patriarchs and the prophets seems to have been dispelled — for centuries of waiting have passed, and the centuries of certitude have arrived. The apostles no longer content themselves with hope ; they have faith. The handsome visage of Saint Andrew breathes a profound calm. On all these faces there is the stamp of nobility of the soul and serenity of the spirit. They conjure up the portrait of Saint Bartholomew that one finds in the writings of the Pseudo-Abdias : "His face is clear, his eyes large, his nose straight and regular. His abundant beard is streaked with a few white hairs. For twenty years he has been wearing the same clothes, yet they have not become worn out or soiled. Angels accompany him on his travels. He always has the same serene and affable countenance. He speaks the language of all men, and he knows what I am saying at this moment"[11]. It was at Chartres that the apostles appeared for the first time with this moral beauty ; fashioned by the word of their Master, they resemble him. At Chartres, Christ is in their midst, his statue standing against the pier. He also is revealed with quite another aspect. No longer is he the distant God of Romanesque portals, the remote Sovereign of the Apocalypse, the formidable Judge surrounded by the four beasts and the twenty-four Elders : he has come down to earth, and he stands, in order to be closer to mankind. This fine statue is no longer of Christ entered into eternal life, but of Christ made man, the Christ of the parables and the Sermon on the Mount. No doubt it was entrusted to the greatest sculptor in the workshop — its technique differs only slightly from that of the apostles, but a master has left his mark there : the longer face is more noble, the unlined brow radiates more light, and there is more gentleness in the eyes.

The Christ and the apostles at Chartres aroused great admiration, and for twenty years artists came to study these great works as models. It is possible that they inspired the apostles of the central portal and the Christ on the pier at Notre-Dame in Paris, which today are destroyed. The apostles and the Christ on the northern portal at Reims, so different in style, are nonetheless related by their attributes. At Amiens, where this type of art reaches its maturity, the apostles still retain more than one trace of the original model. The "handsome God" of Amiens copied the one at Chartres with a masterly nobility, without forgetting its gentle, evangelical spirit.

The tympanum of the Last Judgment is conceived with an unparalleled clarity : Christ, seated like a judge, is bare breasted, and raises his hands to show his wounds,

10. On the northern façade, the prophets Elijah and Elisha are added to the series of ten prophets and patriarchs, but they are outside the portal on the wall. I give the two statues of Saint Simon and Saint Matthew their traditional names, without being absolutely certain of their identity.

11. This passage from the Pseudo-Abdias has been reproduced in the *Legende dorée : de sancto Bartholomeo.*

reminding men of the grandeur of his sacrifice ; around the throne, angels kneel or fly in the heavens, carrying the instruments of his Passion, and the wounds, nails, lance and crown of thorns, accuse against all those who have turned away from their Redeemer. Now all has been accomplished, and on the lintel, Saint Michael, the grave archangel of justice, standing on the threshold of good and evil between the chosen and the damned, weighs their merits and their faults in his scales. There still rests a gleam of hope for the sinners, since the Virgin and Saint John, seated and with folded hands on the right and left of Christ, beseech his mercy for the very last time. Grace is stronger than law. It was believed that on the Day of Judgment, Notre-Dame would save the man who, at the supreme moment, raised up his spirit to her — an image which must have comforted many souls.

Stylistically, the work is still related to the Triumph of the Virgin on the northern portal ; but several years have passed, and the folds in the drapery are already less finely pleated. A delightful idea, seen on the northern portal, reappears on the portal of the Last Judgment : a frieze of angels separates the tympanum from the lintel. Here, the angels form two distinct groups : to the right of Saint Michael they welcome the chosen few, and seem to open up the heavens to them ; to the left, they chase the damned towards the open jaws of Leviathan, the symbol of Hell[12]. At Chartres, these two throngs of souls, separated by divine decree, are governed by a depth of feeling which has no place for violent gestures. The chosen, their hands clasped in prayer, their heads raised towards the heavens, radiate a joy whose immensity as yet knows no bounds ; the damned, wringing their hands, are forced in stupefied dismay towards the gulf by the angels. The artists had so much to say that they began on the tympanum and lintel, and continued their story on the lower part of the voussoirs. They showed the dead, with shrouded faces and folded hands, upright in their tombs, dazzled by the broad daylight of eternity. Abraham welcoming the souls of the just in his arms, the chosen, appareled in their celestial bodies guided towards the heavens by angels ; on the side of the reprobates, they showed the great woman of the Apocalypse forced to succumb to hideous demons, and the courtesan dragged upside down on the back of a devil, her long hair sweeping the ground. The lack of proportion and the clumsy rendering of the naked bodies is sometimes shocking, but the verve and creative power are admirable. This must have been the reaction of the sculptors of the Last Judgment at Reims, as they borrowed more than one original idea from the artists at Chartres.

A vivid contrast exists between these scenes of the Last Judgment, where the artists' imagination is given free rein, and the solemnity of the voussoirs. The angels are ranked there in the order given by Dionysus the Areopagite in the fifth century, in his *Celestial Hierarchy*. This famous book translated in the ninth century from Greek into Latin by Scotus Erigenus completely dominated all medieval thought ; here, the invisible world is described with the precision and the magnificence that would reappear later in Dante. The nine choirs of angels form great concentric circles around God, and their brightness grows as they approach the source of light. At Chartres one recognises the Seraphim, the Cherubim, the Thrones, the Dominions, the Virtues, the Powers, the Principalities, the Archangels and the Angels. The Seraphim, nearest to the source of all heat and all brightness hold balls of fire in their hands, while the Cherubim who follow them hold flames. This learned hierarchy shows the care taken by the clergy at Chartres to define a predetermined plan of work for their artists.

This Last Judgment portal, so abundant with life and thought, must have been in place by 1212. This was (apparently) the year when the marriage of Pierre de Dreux and Alix de Bretagne took place. In effect, on the pier beneath the feet of the statue of Christ the teacher, the couple may be seen at table, with their servants getting ready the customary baskets of bread to distribute to the poor. This, the most beautiful statue of the portal was probably sculpted last, and was a gift from the great family of Drieux-Bretagne, whose generosity would be so important for Chartres[13].

---

12. These angels who appear at half length above the mixed group of the chosen and the damned produced such an excellent effect that they were copied at Amiens by the sculptor of the Last Judgment.
13. The hypothesis that Pierre de Droux and his wife Alix de Bretagne may be recognised beneath the feet of Christ, is very probably correct. They were the donors of the rose window and the lancets of the southern façade, a little later. At Reims, the drapers, the donors of the statue of Christ on the northern portal, are also sculpted beneath his feet.

The Triumph of the Virgin and the Last Judgment portals, which had been planned from the start, were the first to be completed.

While work was in progress on them however, an even greater project was conceived, and two new portals were opened on each transept façade, as has been mentioned. There are such striking stylistic parallels between these two portals that one may confidently suppose that they were executed within a short space of time, one after the other, often by the same artists. It is quite obvious that the draperies of the Christ crowned in glory of the tympanum and the two angels accompanying him are closely related to those of Christ, the Virgin, Saint John and the angels of the Last Judgment. The tall statues of the martyrs in the splays sometimes show surprising analogies with the apostle statues. The two martyrs, Saint Laurence and Saint Vincent resemble the still archaic countenance of the apostle Saint John, in the shape of their faces and the style of their hair and beards ; and the martyr who is given the name Saint Piat hardly differs from the apostle Saint Thomas. The same stage in technique and thought is demonstrated here, and it is difficult to refrain from giving these portals very similar dates. These parallels are felt all the more strongly in that the two statues of Saint George and Saint Theodore, added afterwards, announce a new style.

The tympanum on this portal is extraordinary, and at first appears inexplicable. Christ, with a crown on his head is *standing* between two kneeling angels, and holds a palm branch in his hand[14]. What is the meaning of this unusual image ? The scenes sculpted on the lintel and on the voussoirs offer the explanation. They represent Saint Stephen in discussion with the Jews, dragged forward by his executioners and finally stoned. The martyr dies "Looking up steadfastly into heaven and sees the glory of God" while he utters these words : "Behold, I see the heavens opened, and the Son of man *standing* on the right hand of God"[15]. This text from the *Acts of the Apostles* explains the Christ on the tympanum.

The figures arranged in rows on the voussoirs are martyrs. Holy Innocents who marked the beginning of the era of bloody sacrifices are ranked the first, and are seated on thrones. Then come the martyrs of the Apocalypse, recognisable thanks to the river of blood which escapes from a lamb's head placed at the summit of the voussoir, and which runs down onto their tunics. They are the martyrs who have "washed their robes... in the blood of the Lamb"[16]. The martyrs on the other voussoirs are arranged in a hierarchy and rise from deacon to priest, from priest to bishop, and from bishop to pope.

Nearly all these large statues may be named without difficulty. Saint Stephen may be recognised by his gentle face, for he appeared as "beautiful as an angel" to the members of the Sanhedrin ; and he may also be recognised by the Jewish doctor beneath his feet. The pope Saint Clement has the submerged church of La Cheronèse as his pedestal — his relics were interred there. The deacon next to Saint Stephen can only be Saint Laurence, as they were inseparable for the Middle Ages, and were said to be united in the same tomb. Saint Vincent is characterised by the crow on his pedestal which defends his corpse against a wolf, and Saint Denis by the lion he tamed in the arena by making the sign of the cross. The name of the priest next to Saint Denis alone gives rise to some doubt. Some have affirmed that it is Saint Piat, the apostle from Tournai, whose relics were brought to Chartres at the time of the Norman invasions and were especially venerated there. The hypothesis is very sound, but cannot be presumed fact.

All these statues are as solemn and as rigid as those of the apostles, but they are less austere. The priestly ornaments, the stoles, the embroidered bands along the bottoms of the tunics, the bindings of the books carried by the deacons — all are treated with a rare delicacy, and add a touch of refined decoration to the simplicity of ecclesiastical dress.

The statues of the two martyred soldiers, Saint George and Saint Theodore were added a little after the others on either side of the portal and are in strong contrast to them. They are still immobile, but no longer rigid, and for the first time they show simple, lifelike lines. A hand grips a lance or holds a shield in a perfectly natural manner, and the feet rest solidly not on a figure but on a pedestal. The simplicity of the fine

14. Only a few traces of it remain.
15. *Acts*, VII, 56.
16. *Revelation*, VII, 14.

apparel of the thirteenth century knight harmonises with the simplicity of the pose. The art of the thirteenth century suddenly appears to attain perfection. Yet few years separate these statues from their neighbours, and certain features draw them closer. Saint George's hair and beard still curl in scrolls like the hair and beard of Saint Peter on the Last Judgment portal ; Saint Theodore belongs to the family of deacons on the Martyr portal, with slightly more refined features. There are no more than seven or eight years between the two series. The date 1218 or 1220, probably the same as for that other masterpiece, the Coronation of the Virgin at Notre-Dame in Paris, would seem suitable for these two sculptures at Chartres. This solemn moment marks the appearance of a new classical art in Christian Europe. These two statues of martyrs are not only masterpieces, but great figures in the annals of French history and poetry. Saint George who wears the beard of a fighting soldier is one of those barons fresh from his combat at the side of Philippe-Auguste at Bouvines, where France was saved. As for

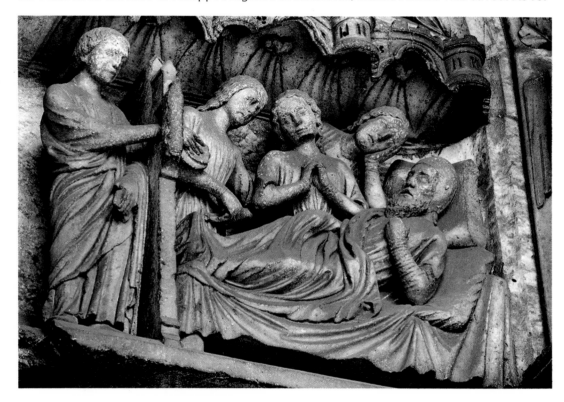

82. South portal, Confessors' bay. Tympanum. Saint Nicholas gives his purse to the impoverished nobleman.

Saint Theodore, young and handsome, courageous and gentle, he is the purest type of knight, concieved and moulded by the Church and by contemporary poetry. Thus the sculptors at Chartres gave their subjects a contemporary sensibility.

**The south façade.
The confessors portal**

The Confessors' portal must have been started in 1212, at the time when the two other portals were nearing completion. The six large statues in the splays, with their archaic poses, are certainly earlier than those of Saint George and Saint Theodore. A superficial glance would imply that there are no differences between them and the statues on the Martyr portal, for everything seems identical : the delicately embroidered ecclesiastical garments, the arms clasped to the body, the restrained gestures, or the feet balanced on small figures of men or of animals. A more careful examination reveals certain differences in style : the short beard is no longer treated in terms of masses, but indicated by a few light tufts and lines ; the same goes for the hair. There is one far more striking innovation however : three of these figures are no longer general types, but express temperament and character. Saint Martin, the apostle of Gaul, radiates both strength and goodness ; with his head raised high, he looks towards the distant regions he will conquer with his faith. If one reads the life of Saint Martin, it would be difficult to imagine him with a nobler countenance. Saint Jerome makes a striking contrast with this missionary and man of action : small, contemplative, carrying a book and a scroll of parchment, he is the scholar, the learned man, shut in his cell with the Bible he translates, and which he carried off from the Synagogue because it had become incapable of comprehending the biblical message[17]. Saint Gregory the Great has the spiritualised face of an ascetic, and the inner radiance of the man of inspiration. He listens to the dove of the Holy Spirit which has perched on his shoulder[18]. The artistic forms which up to this point had so magnificently expressed the idea of the apostle, the patriarch and the prophet, elevated to a type, began to quicken with life and to portray the particular features of an individual Saint. The three other statues have less personality and are more difficult to name. It may be conceded that Saint Nicholas corresponds to Saint Martin, as both are depicted on the tympanum. It is possible that Saint Leon corresponds to Saint Gregory, for in Rome the two great popes were sometimes linked together. However, to suppose that Saint Ambrose is the pendant to Saint Jerome is a matter of pure conjecture[19].

Two statues were added later onto the confessor series, those of Saint Avit and Saint Laumer who were particularly venerated at Chartres, and each of whom had founded a monastery in the Merovingian period. Both bore the stamp of the mature artistic style of Reims cathedral. Saint Avit's head bears a strange resemblance to the head of the famous prophet at Reims (sometimes compared to Ulysses), whose drapery is classical but whose face is unmistakably French. Its large face is constructed in the same way, and the beard as well as the hair is identical in style, made up of elegant drilled scrolls. If the prophet at Reims is approximately dated 1250 — the general opinion — Saint Avit could only be dated a few years later. These two statues, strangers to the Chartres workshop, are the final additions to the cathedral exterior.

The tympanum of the Confessors' portal was sculpted after the six oldest statues and is significantly different from those which have been studied up to this point. It is the work of a sculptor who was both daring and capable of great delicacy. The tympanum he conceived substitutes a feeling for the picturesque for the expression of grandeur. Five different compartments containing four different stories replace the figure or solemn group which normally forms the centre of the composition, while dominant horizontal lines reinforce the impression of novelty. Three people lie in bed in three of the compartments, while a horse in profile is placed in the centre of the fourth. This tympanum is divided up into the stories of Saint Martin and Saint Nicholas. On the left, Saint Martin gives half his military cloak to the poor man. Then, during the night, he has a dream in which Christ, surrounded by angels, reveals himself to the saint, wearing this portion of the cloak[20]. On the right, Saint Nicholas throws a purse into the bedroom of a high ranking figure, fallen into such penury that he is on the point of abandoning his three daughters to lives of dishonour. Above, the famous tomb of Saint Nicholas at Bari is depicted, with its never-ending stream of oil whose powers heal the sick. This is not all however, for the story continues below on the voussoirs. Here the sculptor tells the story of Saint Giles. The hermit saint is seen with a wounded hand, defending the hind, which nourished him with her milk, from the king's huntsmen. He is then seen celebrating Mass in the presence of Charlemagne, and holding a parchment, brought down by an angel, he reads the sin which the emperor dared not avow during confession.

This portal leads the imagination forward on the great pilgrimage routes. Saint Martin of Tours, and Saint Giles of the Languedoc were two stages on the pilgrimage to Saint James of Compostella, and Bari had been one of the holy places for Christianity ever since Saint Nicholas's relics had been brought there from Asia Minor.

This tympanum with its divisions and its episodes in the lives of saints is the work of an artist skilled in conveying detail. Saint Martin, who is sleeping with one leg crossed and his hand on his cheek, has a supple elegance. The three young girls, destined by their father to lives of shame, have fine faces hollowed by hunger and veiled with

17. Beneath his feet is the Synagogue personified, with a blindfold on her eyes. She does not know how to interpret the book which has been left in her care.
18. On the pedestal we see Saint Gregory's scribe, who one day, through a slit in the curtain saw the dove speaking into his ear.
19. It is difficult to believe that the crowned figure beneath the saint's feet, and whom he spears with his cross, is the Emperor Maxime whose conduct was daringly reproved by Saint Ambrose, on his way from Trèves. It is more likely to be a persecutor or a heretic.
20. Christ wearing the cloak takes up the topmost compartment. This completes the compartment representing the dream of Saint Martin.

sadness. These emaciated faces full of grace despite their melancholy, seem to herald a new art and are just one of the secrets of this sculptor who was so evidently refined and sensitive. His style may occasionally be traced on the voussoirs. As with the other portals, these voussoirs are arranged according to the rules of ecclesiastical hierarchy. The confessors who were sanctified by the Church may be seen here, together with those who were sanctified through the passage of time. Each one has his place in the Church's ranks, and the subdeacon, the deacon, the priest, the bishop, the archbishop and the pope may be recognised in turn. The pope and the emperor, keystones of society, are positioned at the top of the voussoirs. These statuettes were in place in 1224, when, with the portals finished, it was decided that the southern façade should be made more handsome by the addition of a porch[21].

The north façade. The Old Testament portal

The two portals of the northern transept, which frame the Triumph of the Virgin portal must have been built at an early date, but remained undecorated for quite some time. All the evidence would suggest that they were the last to be completed.

The sculptors must have started work on the Old Testament portal some time around 1220. A curious mixture of tradition and innovation characterises the ensemble, for not a single one of these six portals fails to convey a sense of creative effort. New thoughts were constantly developing and inspiration always alert amongst the sculptors, for whom imitation was the principle of progress, and the admiration of one's fellow artists the ultimate achievement.

The tall biblical statues, selected by a theologian, were equally prefigurations of Christ or the Virgin. Baalam standing on his ass prefigures the star above the manger, and the Queen of Sheba, with her neighbour Solomon, prefigures the Adoration of the Magi. This theme is recognisable thanks to the negro depicted on the pedestal who bears gold in a gourd, while beneath Solomon's feet the ironic Marcoul plays a medieval Sancho Panza to the king's Don Quixote, replying to each of the philosopher-king's noble thoughts with his down-to-earth common sense, expressed in trivial proverbs. Joseph, sold by his brothers for thirty pieces of siver, heralds Christ's betrayal by Judas ; Judith triumphing over Holofernes prefigures the Virgin's conquest of sin. Finally Jesus, son of Sirach, who looks down at the building of the temple of Jerusalem, is a figure of that other Jesus who founded the Church.

These statues are linked to the past by several features. They remain attached to the architecture and are rarely out of vertical alignment. They hold ribbons inscribed with their names against their chests, and stand on pedestals formed by small human or animal figures.

Two statues, however, stand out because of the freedom of their pose : the Queen of Sheba and Solomon. The Queen of Sheba holds her cape by a cord with one hand, and the folds of her dress in the other, without moving her arms away from her body. Such natural gestures herald the great art of the thirteenth century. The rounded heads differ from all those previously discussed, as if a new sculptor is asserting his presence. Those long faces which suggested an ancient race of men, remote from reality, are no more, and the sense of distant historical time is no longer insistent. The Queen of Sheba is an amiable princess from the Ile-de-France : she is no longer the Queen of solitude. Judith alone retains something of the grandeur of the Old Testament, in her long pleated robe and veils.

On the tympanum, however, in contrast, there is work of a completely biblical inspiration by another artist. Job lies almost naked, on a dungheap strewn with snail shells, in the grip of a hideous demon who plants one of his claws in Job's skull and one in the sole of his foot. This is the translation of the verse : "Satan smote Job with sore boils from the sole of his foot unto his crown[22]." The patriarch's face remains impassive, ravaged with furrows as though it had been sculpted by rain, while he scrapes his ulcers with a potsherd. Indifferent to his friend's arguments, to the pleadings of his wife, he retains an unshakeable confidence in the Eternal God, who appears above his head. This Job, sculpted at Chartres so long ago, is almost as grandiose a figure as the biblical Job himself. The statue, which aroused great admiration — with every good reason — was

21. A charming statuette, whose tunic had horizontally pleated folds, must have been added later, at the same time as the statues of Saint Avit and Saint Laumer were sculpted.

22. *Job, II, 7.*

84. North porch,
central bay voussoirs.
The Creation :
the separation of the waters,
the plants,
the sun and the moon,
the fish and the birds.

85. North porch,
central bay voussoirs.
Adam and Eve.

86-87. North porch,
Confessor's bay voussoirs.
The Active life
and the Contemplative life.

imitated a few years later on one of the northern portals at Reims cathedral, by an artist who was more skilful, but of lesser stature altogether.

The lintel depicts the Judgment of Solomon, a swift drama, conceived with perfect clarity. Solomon has just given the order to divide the child in two, and a black courtier draws his sword. The false mother accepts the sentence saying : "Let it be neither thine nor mine." But the true mother, her hands covering her face, can scarcely contain her grief, and gives the pathetic cry which has echoed movingly down the centuries : "Oh my Lord, give her the living child, and in no wise slay it[23]." Instantly Solomon discerned the true meaning of the lie ; he stretched out his hand and ordered the servant carrying the child to give it back to its mother. The elders of Israel sitting near the tribunal, admired their young king's decision, and recognised the wisdom he had acquired through alloting the child.

Creative genius rules over the spirit of tradition in the voussoirs. The narrative on the tympanum and the lintel of the three portals of the south façade was seen to continue on the horizontal voussoirs below, but the remaining voussoirs were reserved for the hierarchy of angels or of saints. The voussoirs rested in the realm of the heavens. On the Old Testament portal, however, only the first band depicts angels. Certain of them, charged by God to guide the stars in their courses carry the sun, moon and the stars. The other voussoirs each contain a narrative : each is symbolic and intented to arouse thoughts of Christ or the Virgin. Thus when Samson bursts open the gates of Gaza one must recognise Christ opening the door of his tomb : the dew bathing Gideon's fleece symbolises divine grace descending on the Virgin ; in Esther and Judith saving Israel, the Mother of God is seen bringing salvation to the world ; Tobias's son restoring his old father's vision represents Christ opening men's eyes to the light.

Certain of these small scenes are quite beautiful. Esther kneels before Ahasuerus with a touching humility as she begs him for mercy towards her people. Before leaving for Bethulia, Judith is seen in her house, covering her head with ashes and praying fervently ; she reappears leaving the town, and walking towards Holofernes' camp, confident in her beauty. The young Tobias kneels before his father restoring his sight with the fish's gall, and the old man, waiting for the light, tenderly presses his son's head against his breast ; the dog seems to be waiting too, and the angel stays too, to witness the miracle. As each voussoir could hold only two or three figures, the sculptor had to learn to condense the narrative imaginitively, and to give the episodes of the story a clear order. He was often able to create an imposing impression with small figures, and just as the rules of poetry give rise so often to works of perfect beauty, these architectural constraints were the driving force behind new innovations.

The north façade. The Virgin portal

The most striking aspect of the Virgin portal is the contrast between the archaic character of the tympanum and the stylistic perfection of the large statues, a contrast which suggests that work on the portal was started extremely early and came to a halt, before being recommenced at a much later date : the tympanum appears to have been sculpted in 1210 and the tall statues in 1225 or thereabouts. Of all the statues on the six portals, the beautiful Annunciation and Visitation scenes were the last to be sculpted, though the statues of Saint Avit and Saint Laumer are later.

The tympanum is archaic not only as regards its style but also the choice of subject matter. It depicts themes typical of both Romanesque and early Gothic portals dedicated to the Virgin Mary[24] : the Nativity, the Annunciation to the Shepherds, and the Adoration of the Magi. One significant feature relates V-MS Judgment portals, the oldest portals of the transept ; a frieze of angels, depicted half-lengh, separates the top of the lintel from the tympanum. This was the sole artistic liberty taken with a traditionally rigid design scheme, and as a motif it was abandoned on the portals constructed at a later date.

In contrast with the tympanum, which repeats the formulas of the past, some of the tall statues differ from all those previously discussed, and are in fact very forward looking, in their daring break with architectural tradition. In the Annunciation scene, the angel and the Virgin Mary face each other, engaged in a dialogue that is between

88. North porch, central bay. Detail of vault.

23. *I Kings*, III, 16-28.
24. For this subject, see *L'art religieux du XIIe siècle en France*, pp. 426 ff.

89. South portal,
central bay.
Christ the teacher.

90. South porch
and towers.

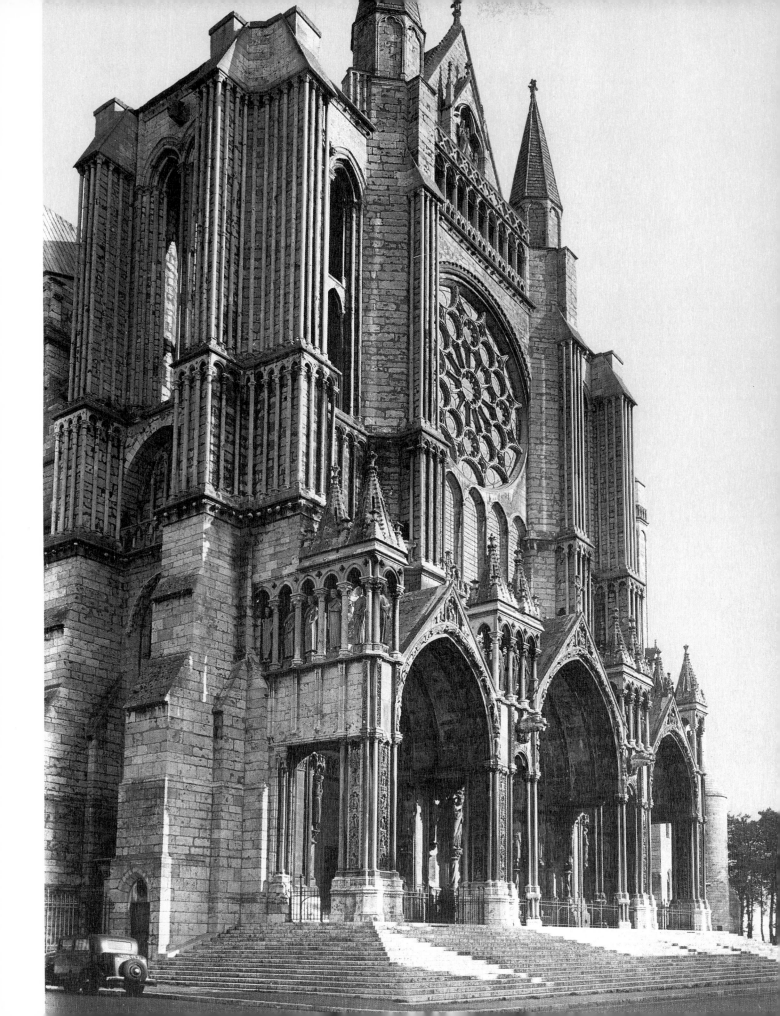

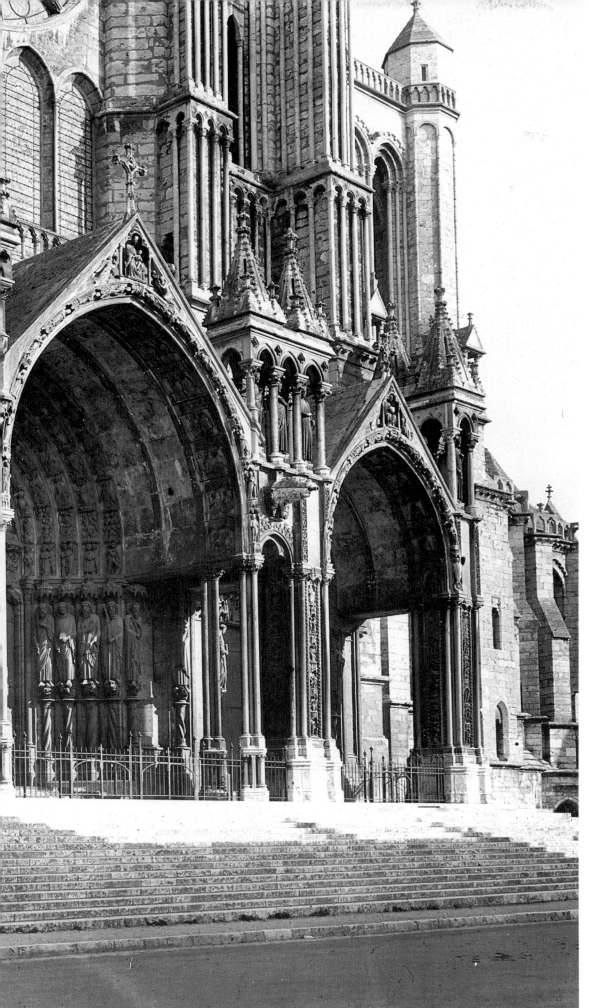

91. South porch,
central bay
depicting Christ,
flanked by Confessor's bay
on left
and Martyrs' bay
on right.

heaven and earth. The Visitation scene contains another innovation : Mary and Elizabeth greet each other with arms outstretched. For the first time the arms are extended away from the chest. So a quarter of a century had to elapse before life and movement were granted to the column figure. Then, however, the feet of the statue were given a proper base on pedestals.

The small symbolic statues appear this time beneath the socles as opposed to the feet of the tall figures. The Virgin of the Annunciation stands above the burning bush, and the Virgin of the Visitation above the Serpent of Eden. Four of these statues, the angel, the Virgin of the Annunciation and the two prophets, chosen from all those who foretold the motherhood of Christ, share various common features with the biblical statues ot the Old Testament portal previously described. Two, however, have a different appearance : the Virgin of the Visitation and Saint Elizabeth. They appear clothed in light because of the shallower folds in their clothing. The Virgin's long tunic gives an impression of purity, reminiscent of the mysterious tunic hidden away in the holy reliquary, which the artist must have had in mind when he gave the sculpture such long, fluid lines. Saint Elizabeth has a pose reminiscent of the classical funerary statues which could still be encountered along Roman roads near city gates. This style retains a certain modesty, however, which corresponds with the chaste features of the statues and is altogether less confident, less pronounced that its classical counterpart. True masterpieces, these statues were copied almost immediately, and echoes of Chartres' Saint Elizabeth may be seen in Saint Eutropia, sister of Saint Nicaise on the north portal at Reims cathedral, which depicted local saints of the diocese. Saint Eutropia wears the same veil on her head, over the same wavy hair as Saint Elizabeth, and her drapery falls in a similar fashion. She is not so tall, her features are more strained and her dress has deeper folds, it is true, but the relationship is evident. The tall statues on the façade at Amiens cathedral reproduce the conversation between the Virgin Mary and the angel, and the Virgin and Saint Elizabeth, from Chartres[25]. They reappear with magnificent proportions on the west façade of Reims cathedral in 1250 or thereabouts. The famous portals at Chartres were to remain a model for many years, and sculptors came from far and wide to study them.

The voussoirs on this portal celebrate the perfections of the Virgin through symbol or allusion. The Wise Virgins of the parable stand opposite the Foolish Virgins, and the twelve virtues, "fruits of the Holy Spirit", enumerated by Saint Paul, are represented here like ornaments adorning Notre Dame. One band of voussoirs depicts the triumph of the Virtues over the Vices, a curious work, in that it is the last reminiscence of Aurelius Prudentius Clemens' *Psychomachia*. In this well known poem, composed towards the end of the fourth century, Prudentius told the story of the battle of the Virtues and the Vices, a subject artists had depicted for many centuries.

At Chartres, the battle is over : the Virtues have the Vices at their feet. Certain features evoke definite moments in the poem. In front of Humility, Pride rolls in the ditch which gapes before him. Beneath Charity, Avarice hides her treasure in her bosom, and at Hope's feet, Despair pierces hercelf with a sword. Despite these references, however, a new conception of the battle of the Virtues and the Vices is felt. This is developed on the south porch.

The porches.
The south porch

The sculptural wealth of the cathedral was increased when the south porch was begun in 1224. The vaults were supported with four sturdy pillars decorated on all four sides with bas-reliefs. Apparently, the first of these to be sculpted depicted the Virtues and the Vices, following the recent example of the series on the lower part of the Last Judgment portal at Notre-Dame in Paris[26]. Their appearance was entirely novel. The Virtues are shown as majestically seated women who bear an emblem or heraldic beast on their coats of arms, symbolising their nobility. The Vices were no longer personified, but represented in action : a lady of the manor beating her servant represented Violence, and a monk, unfrocking himself at the monastery door represented Inconstancy. In this way virtue was characterised by its essence and vice through its effects. These calm female figures demonstrated that virtue brought peace to the soul, while

92. South portal, central bay. Last Judgment.

25. These statues were sculpted between 1225 and 1235.
26. A few of these bas-reliefs at Paris have been slightly disfigured by eighteenth century restoration work.

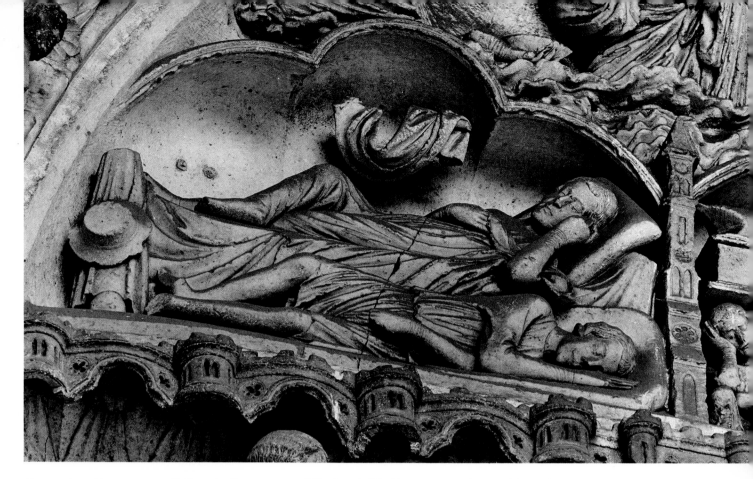

the contrasting scenes of disorderliness proved that outside there was only trouble and turmoil. The bas-reliefs at Notre-Dame in Paris, with their elaborate design scheme[27] provoked great admiration at the time, for they were imitated after a short interval at Chartres and at Amiens. The Chartres series seems earlier than the one at Amiens as the Virtues look graver and are sometimes more archaic in style. As the twelve Virtues had to oppose the twelve Vices, it seemed obvious to decorate the face of each pillar with six bas-reliefs. The bas-reliefs on the four pillars of the porch were thus determined in principle as to their number, dimensions, and positioning by those at Notre-Dame in Paris. Similarly, the Virtues and the Vices were depicted in relationship to the Last Judgment portal. Their twenty-four images covered half the surface of the two central pillars. To fill the remaining twenty-four places, the designer naturally thought of the twenty-four Elders of the Apocalypse, whose presence completed the celestial hierarchy surrounding the Sovereign Judge. They were created several years after the Vices, by accomplished sculptors who used very refined techniques.

The two pillars at the far end of each porch were decorated with twenty-four scenes of martyrdom and twenty-four episodes in the lives of the Confessors. These were not bas-reliefs, but small figures arranged similarly to those on the voussoirs. The drama, reduced to essentials, as a rule involves only two figures. In the thirteenth century there was reluctance to represent either physical suffering or violent feeling in art; accordingly the martyrs march serenely to their punishment; the executioners themselves remain calm, and no trace of bestiality shows on their faces. The murderers who assassinate Saint Thomas à Becket strike him without hate or anger, and Saint Sernin of Toulouse, dragged down the Capitol steps, maintains the impassivity of a statue.

It is not always easy to recognise the martyr or confessor whose story is dramatised here in stone. Their traditional names are correct as a rule[28], but certain attributions are questionable and some of these heros of faith must remain unidentified. Clearly the intention was to perpetuate the names of the saints of the Chartres area and neighbouring regions. For example Saint Lubin, a former bishop of Chartres, is

93. South portal,
Confessors' bay.
The stories of Saint Martin
and Saint Nicholas.

94. South portal,
Confessors' bay.
Saint Martin asleep.

27. I have studied them in detail in *L'art religieux du XIIIᵉ siècle en France,* volume III.
28. These names may be found in the *Monographie de la cath. de Chartres* by Abbé Bulteau, vol. II, pp. 361 ff.

95. South portal,
Confessor's bay.
Saint Nicholas.

seen healing Saint Caletric, his future successor. Saint Martin, who was responsible for two miracles at Chartres is commemorated, and the hermit Saint Carilef (Saint Calais) is rescued from oblivion. His holiness drew animals and the birds of the air to his side, and one day, while he was digging his garden, a wren laid its eggs in the tunic he had hung on an oak tree, so seeking the saint's protection. This charming narrative is depicted quite clearly on the confessors' pillar.

Chartres sought subjects far beyond familiar horizons, however, taking in the whole of Christendom. Side by side with local saints appear those whose cult was widespread — celebrated martyrs, great popes, Fathers of the Church, famous monks and anchorites, for example Saint Benoit of Subiaco, and Saint Antony, with his faun in the desert. Curiously enough, amongst all these saints, not one is female. None of the touching female martyrs of Rome, Gaul or Africa, no female saints of France or the Orient appear on these pillars. They are not to be seen on the voussoirs of the portals, and not one of them has her statue among the group of confessors and martyrs[29]. For at Chartres, female saints were forgotten in the presence of Notre-Dame, who outshone them all. This porch is the proof : an examination of the groups decorating the three gables reveals the Virgin in majesty with the Child on her knees in the centre, the Virgin again on the right, this time enthroned, and welcoming an angel who presents her with the sceptre of royal queens, and on the left, finally, Saint Anne, the Virgin's mother, bearing a lily in a vase which is the symbol of her daughter's immaculate nature. Still higher up, a series of pinnacles decorated with eighteen statues of kings may be observed. The first of these is David, holding in his hand the stem of the genealogical tree which grows from the breast of Jesse, who lies at his feet. These eighteen kings are thus the kings of Judah, ancestors of the Virgin Mary, and they were placed here in her honour. In this way the south façade with its absence of female saints culminates with the Triumph of the Virgin.

The construction of the north porch closely followed that of the south porch. It is lighter in style, however, and not so richly decorated. Statues are supported on pedestals in column form, always elegant, but whimsically designed at times. Their number has been reduced, as a few were broken during the French Revolution. Fortunately the destruction which began on this side of the cathedral was almost immediately brought to a halt.

The north porch, its statues and statuettes

It was long believed that these statues represented the cathedral's benefactors. Philippe-Auguste, Saint Louis and his sister Isabelle, Richard the Lionheart, Saint Ferdinand of Castile, Philippe, Count of Boulogne and his wife the countess Mahaut were blithely named at random, without a trace of proof. This was the period when it was believed that historical figures could be counted as the physical descendants of Jesus Christ so it was thought that William the Conqueror and Queen Matilda could be recognised on the Portail Royal[30]. Surprisingly the small sculpted scenes beneath the statues in the north porch did not provide enlightenment. Episodes in the stories of David and Saul may be deciphered beneath the feet of the so-called Philippe-Auguste and Richard the Lionheart, [31] proving that two kings of Judah are sculpted here rather than a king of France and a king of England. Two small bas-reliefs tell the story of Samuel ; and Samuel, his mother Hannah, his father Elkanah and the high priest Eli are all named by inscriptions. Everything would indicate, therefore, that the four large statues above the bas-reliefs represent Samuel, Hannah, Elkanah and the high priest Eli holding his censer. All these north porch statues are thus figures from the Old Testament, who prophesy the coming of Christ or the Virgin, with two exceptions. These are Saint Potentien, who according to legend spread Christianity in the Chartres region, and Saint Modeste, daughter of the Governer Quirinus, who was converted on listening to Saint Potentien and suffered martyrdom with him. After their conspicuous

29. The porch was decorated with bands of statuettes, which seemed to be the continuation of the voussoirs of the portals. These statuettes represent the apostles, the patriarchs, the prophets, the Wise and the Foolish Virgins and the angels. One of these bands consists of fourteen female figurines, each with a crown and holding a flower in her hand. It is very difficult to decide whether these should be seen as the Virtues, the Beatitudes or saints. If they were saints, it would be impossible to name them.
30. Abbé Bulteau, *op. cit.* vol. 1, pp. 65 ff.
31. These two statues have been destroyed.

absence on the south porch, a female saint is finally found here on the north porch, providing, incidentally, an approximate date for its construction, as Saint Modeste was imitated on the portal of Amiens cathedral between 1225 and 1235.

Several of these statues are inexplicably mediocre in quality, but many are of captivating beauty. Saint Modeste is a masterpiece of graceful chastity. The high priest Eli, with his bare forehead and flowing beard, vies in ecclesiastical magnificence with the biblical patriarchs on the central portal. The beautiful Old Testament heroine, tall and slightly aloof, simply dressed in the noble style of the times of Blanche of Castile, is the perfect image of the great thirteenth century lady.

Bands of statuettes decorate the porch, and on the voussoirs of the right hand arch the signs of the zodiac and the works of each month may be seen, evidently a rather free imitation of the beautiful calendar on the Coronation of the Virgin portal at Notre-Dame de Paris, though it lacks the original's special character.

The story of the Creation and the Fall of Man provides a powerful subject, grandly treated, for the archivolt of the central arch. According to the theologians, not God but his Word, Jesus Christ, created the world, which explains Christ's presence here for each day of creation. He raises his hand to draw creatures out of the void, and occasionally blesses them, for the Holy fathers say that the world was created through love. A mysterious figure seems to be present at the origin of the world : seated, with his hand on his cheek, thoughtful and rather haggard, he wears a Jewish skull cap, and has a book on his knees. It is Moses, who appears to be contemplating the wondrous power of divine might with awe and terror. This extraordinary figure, unique in the history of art, appears to be the witness as well as the historian of the origins of the world[32].

These voussoirs of the Creation and the Fall are often moving in their beauty. Adam is still half mingled with the earth, but God has already fashioned the upper part of his body, and like a sculptor he models his face in clay. Man thenceforth would bear the mark of the hand of the great Artist on his forehead. There is nothing more touching than the sight of Adam after he has sinned. He is the image of despair, hidden away in a thicket, one knee on the ground, the other supporting his arm which holds his head, bowed in grief. He listens terrified for the approach of God. It is appropriate to tell the story of the Fall here at such length, for it leads up to the Virgin crowned in glory on the tympanum. Woman's sin leads to her triumph. The voussoirs of the left hand arch of the porch show ten personifications. The first of these voussoirs depicts the Active and the Contemplative life. Six charmingly natural women are shown washing, carding and spinning wool, the others combing flax and winding it in skeins. These symbolise Active life. Six other women opposite, wearing nuns' habits, represent the Contemplative life. One of them has opened the book on her knee, but the others, having finished reading have shut their books to meditate or pray, and the last of the women, who has no book at all, looks up to the heavens and with her head thrown back, abandons herself to religious ecstasy.

The outermost band of voussoirs contains female figures symbolising the blessed state of the body and the soul in eternal life[33]. They should have been placed on the Last Judgment portal near the procession of the chosen few for they are the expression of heavenly bliss, but this felicitous idea only occured to the designer of the scheme much later. According to the doctrine of Saint Anselm[34], which was accepted unanimously by the theologians of the twelfth and thirteenth centuries, imperishable gifts would be bestowed upon the bodies and souls of the blessed on the Day of Judgment. Beauty, equality, strength, liberty, health, sensuality and longevity would be bestowed on the glorified body, while wisdom, friendship, concord, honour, power, security and joy would be bestowed upon the soul. All that man lacked upon earth would be finally his. The soul would be reconciled with the body, and with itself, in a state of pure harmony. These immortal gifts were portrayed with an admirable delicacy of feeling at Chartres, as a choir of fourteen crowned virgins. Some are of the purest elegance, some are not

32. Another strange figure, that of a clean-shaven young man, with a trickle of water apparently running from his hand, is placed next to the Word, creating the birds and the fishes. He is perhaps a personification of the Ocean, who was ordered by God to "bring forth abundantly the moving creature that hath life", *Genesis*, I, 20.
33. Didron, in 1847, thought he recognised the civic virtues here. In 1849, Mme Félicie d'Ayzac demonstrated in her brochure entitled : *Les statues du porche septentrionale de Chartres* that they were beatitudes enjoying eternal life, according to the writings of Saint Anselm.
34. *Patr. lat.*, vol. CXIX, col. 587 and vol. CLVIII, col. 47.

so refined in style, and have less perfect proportions, but all are of interest because of the thoughts they express. With one hand they hold a sceptre and with the other a shield decorated with heraldic devices which enable them to be recognised. Many of them have their names inscribed in stone. Longevity's device is an eagle who grows younger in the fiery rays of the sun. Wisdom has the griffon who knows where to find hidden treasure. Strength bears a lion, Security a fortress, and Beauty roses on her coat of arms. These figures reveals the joys of the chosen few in heaven. Thus the porches reveal the elaboration and the fulfilment of ideas found on the portals.

Chartres cathedral is the most outstanding creation of the Middle Ages. Its west façade demonstrates the perfect flowering of twelfth century sculpture. The north and south façades turn away from the Romanesque tradition and show the birth and initial development of thirteenth century sculpture. At this time, a grave, solemn and profoundly religious sentiment reigned over the statues at Reims cathedral which seem so approachable today. They appear to ignore us, but the spectator is given pause by their beauty and raised to their level of thought. Certain of the statues at Chartres rank among the masterpieces of French art. Unknown, or contemptuously dismissed for two hundred years during the seventeenth and eighteenth centuries, they are today regarded as an essential and magnificent part of France's cultural heritage. Her epic heroes and cathedral saints were both restored to her during the nineteenth and early twentieth centuries. Chartres' finest statues have now become an integral part of the French tradition. Without them the image of France would be incomplete.

96. North portal,
central bay.
Jesse beneath Isaiah's feet.

97. South portal,
central bay.
Apostles.

98. South portal,
central bay.
Apostles.

Pages 130 and 131 :

99. South portal,
Confessors' bay,
Saint Martin, Saint Jerome
and Saint Gregory.

100. South portal,
Confessors' bay.
Saint Leon, Saint Ambrose
and Saint Nicholas.

101. South portal,
Confessors' bay.
Saint Laumer.

102. South portal,
Confessors' bay.
Saint Avit.

103. South portal,
Martyrs' bay.

104. North porch,
Triumph
of the Virgin portal,
flanked
by the Virgin portal
on left,
and the Old Testament portal
on right.

105. North portal,
central bay.
Coronation of the Virgin,
patriarchs and prophets,
prefigurations of Christ.

106. North portal,
central bay.
Moses, Samuel and David.

Pages 138 and 139 :

107. North portal.
Death, Resurrection
and Coronation of the Virgin.

108. North portal,
Old Testament bay.
Job.
The Judgement of Solomon.

137

109. North portal,
central bay.
Saint John the Baptist,
Saint Peter.

110. North portal,
central bay.
Mechizedek and Abraham.

Pages 142 and 143 :

111. North portal,
Virgin bay.
Christ in the crib.
The Adoration of the Magi.

112. North portal,
Virgin bay.
The Visitation.

113. North portal,
Virgin bay.
The Virgin of the Annonciation.

114. North portal,
Old Testament bay.
The story of Gideon,
the life of Judith,
the story of Tobias.

144

Pages 146 and 147 :

115. The three west windows
beneath the rose.

116. West window.
The tree of Jesse, detail

117-118. North portal,
central bay voussoirs.
Tree of Jesse.

Pages 150 and 151 :

119. South rose window.

120. Saint Lubin window, detail.
The wine merchants.

148

5. The stained glass windows

Now that we have studied the huge sculptural decorations of the portals and the porches, we should enter the cathedral itself, where a new world of characters, legends and symbols awaits us.

One hundred and seventy-three sets of stained glass make up the windows and rose windows, a surface area in all of over two thousand square metres; the only omissions being the few panes removed in the eighteenth century to shed more light on the choir, and those destroyed during the Revolution*. All the surviving stained glass windows are the work of thirteenth century artists except for four which escaped the catastrophe of 1194.

The façade with its statues, sculpted from 1145 onwards, was as we have said, spared in the great fire. The three huge windows above the portals with their fragile stained glass remained intact. These three great twelfth century windows are important survivals, and give us the most complete idea of the mastery of these ancient craftsmen. Twelfth century stained glass is rare, and we are very lucky that these windows have been preserved.

They are even more interesting in that one of them contains a still very beautiful, though incomplete, window from the abbey of Saint-Denis. There is now no doubt that these three windows at Chartres are the work of artists who had recently been employed there by Suger[1]. Thus it was not only the sculptors of Saint-Denis who were

121. Clerestory window.

122. Small rose windows, choir.

The twelfth century windows

---

* The stained glass windows of the west façade were restored between 1974 and 1976. (Editor's note.)
1. On this subject see Westlake, *A history of design in painted glass*, London, 4 vols. Folio, 1881. I have studied this question myself in the *Histoire de l'art* by André Michel, Vol.1, p. 786.

summoned to Chartres in 1145 : the master glass-painters came with them and their works all date from the same period. The three windows of the façade represent respectively the tree of Jesse and two scenes from the life of Christ. The first of these two latter windows shows the Childhood of Christ and is dominated by a large figure of the Virgin ; the second begins with the Transfiguration and tells the complete story of the Passion.

The tree of Jesse is an exact reproduction of the one which Suger had made for the basilica of Saint-Denis and which, though damaged and restored, can still be seen there. The conception is grandiose, and may be the work of Suger himself, who was so passionately interested in his church. A great tree springs from Jesse who is lying asleep ; kings sitting one above the other form the trunk of this symbolic tree which terminates with the Virgin Mary : above her Christ is enthroned, surrounded by the seven doves of the Holy Spirit, and on each side of the tree are ranked the Prophets, harbingers of the Messiah throughout the ages. Isaiah's prophecies could not have been translated into images with greater grandeur : "And there shall come forth a rod out of the stem of Jesse, and a branch shall grow out his roots : And the spirit of the Lord shall rest upon him[2]." This beautiful theme, the oldest statement of which is to be found at Saint-Denis, was to be imitated not only at Chartres, but all over France, and soon all over Christendom. Are the other two windows at Chartres also reproductions of originals from Saint-Denis ? We cannot be sure, but there are certain clues that allow us to think so. The Nativity scene, such a new subject at the time, with the Virgin represented lying in bed, and where the Child rests not in a manger but on an altar, seems to have been popularised by the artists trained in Suger's workshops[3].

These three stained glass windows are of the highest technical quality and the borders which surround them are exquisitely decorated[4] ; as for the colour, it is superb. The window representing the Childhood of Christ consists of medallions which are alternately square and circular, with backgrounds of fiery red and deep blue in turn. But the scenes from the Passion window and the figures of the tree of Jesse stand out against a blue of supernatural hue ; as moving as a revelation of another world and deep as an Eastern sky or the finest sapphires. The tree of Jesse, even more perfect than the Passion window, must be the most beautiful piece of existing stained glass.

Another example of twelfth century glass, miraculously saved from the fire, may be seen today in the first window of the southern side aisle of the choir ; it represents the Virgin bearing the Child with majesty in the centre of her breast. For many centuries this Virgin has been deservedly called « Notre-Dame de la belle verrière » or « The Blue Virgin ». The hieratic grandeur of her attitude, the blue of her robe with its rounded folds, and finally the solemn air of the Child make one realize that a twelfth century glass panel has been set into a more recent stained glass window ; for the broad borders decorated with angels as well as the lower parts of the window, where the Wedding at Cana and the Temptation of Christ are illustrated in a different style, bear all the characteristics of thirteenth century art. Here, then, is all that remains of the art of the master glass painters of the twelfth century. There must have been much more, for the documents, doubtless very incomplete, mention eighteen stained-glass windows donated by men of the church before the fire of 1194. Unfortunately, the subjects of these windows are not mentioned.

The thirteenth century windows

The thirteenth century windows constitute the rest of the stained glass of the cathedral. The passing visitor, and even the experts studying them may have difficulty in noticing any significant differences in style between the upper storey, lower storey and rose windows. This appearance of a unified design might make one think that the same workshop produced this vast amount of work in a very short time. It required the undivided critical attention and the continuous vigilance of the canon, M.-Y. Delaporte, to distinguish the nuances of style[5].

2. Isaiah, XI, 1, 2.
3. *L'art religieux du XIIᵉ siècle en France*, pp. 108-9. Note that the Virgin lying in a bed may also be seen on the Portail Royal of Chartres, work of the sculptors from Saint Denis.
4. Those of the Passion window have completely disappeared.
5. The canon, M. Y. Delaporte has written a remarkable work on the stained glass in the cathedral, *Les vitraux de la cathédrale de Chartres*, Chartres, 1926, with three volumes of plates by M. Houvet. He was able to study all the glass at close hand when it was being reinstalled after having been taken down during the war. This is when M. Houvet was able to photograph the windows, and assemble his reproductions in the three volumes which accompany the text.

He distinguished three groups of windows. The first group consists of those of the nave and its side-aisles. These are the oldest, and all probably date from before 1215 ; they are also the finest. The tall male and female saints of the nave windows with their rigid solemnity, their serious look and their beautiful draperies falling around their feet and narrowing like the calyx of a flower, demonstrate the qualities necessary for figures designed to be seen from below and at a great distance. The side aisle windows date from the same period and are sometimes the work of the same artists, but they are conceived in quite a different manner. Here there are no more tall silhouettes, but small figures enclosed in a series of medallions where from close up, beginning at the base (the normal rule), different episodes in the history of a martyr, a confessor or a patriarch may be seen. The arrangement of these small windows shows a perfect respect for such narrative conventions. A few of these windows achieve a high degree of decorative perfection, and occasionally one finds in them an echo of the twelfth century beauty.

The second group consists of the choir windows and those of the ambulatory with its radiating chapels. The choir windows, where several illustrious figures of the thirteenth century are seen kneeling below the saints, must have been executed between 1215 and 1220. Those of the ambulatory and side chapels, though started at the same time, were not finished perhaps until about 1230. These and the others only differ in a few particulars from those of the nave and side aisles ; in each case the ornamental aspects are often less perfect.

The third group is formed by the two great rose windows of the arms of the transept and their accompanying lancet windows. These two magnificent ensembles are almost contemporary and date from about 1230. The northern rose window shows the lilies of France and the towers of Castile : it was a gift from Saint-Louis's mother at the time when her son was still a boy. The rose of the south window is decorated with the arms of Pierre Mauclerc, Count of Dreux, one of the cathedral's great benefactors. The rose window on the west front, with its Last Judgment theme is probably from the same period. Its donor remains anonymous. The stained glass in the naves of the transept was the last to be installed. The windows show the Apostles, and a slight lack of care in the design and less brilliant colours demonstrate a certain haste in the completion of these windows. At Chartres, the work of the stained glass makers went hand in hand with the building programme. The fact that the windows of the nave and the side aisles approach those of the twelfth century in their perfection demonstrates that this part of the cathedral was built first of all, and preceded the choir, whilst the character of the glass of the high transept windows shows this part to be most recent. All this had already been demonstrated to the experts who had made a close study of the architecture.

The donors

All these stained glass windows are gifts, for all the classes of society wanted to contribute to the beauty of the new cathedral, and the whole decorative scheme, completed within almost twenty-five years, is an expression of their faith and love for the Virgin and her church. In the lower part of most of the windows, or in the rose window above them, one or two figures may be seen who are quite separate from the story the artist is telling. Those are the "donor figures", and form what is known as the "signature" of the stained glass. A catalogue of these signatures shows that forty-two windows were given by the craft guilds of the town, forty-four by the great royal and feudal families, sixteen by members of the clergy, and fourteen by figures whose names and social class remain unknown. From first appearances, the clergy seems to have been less generous than the lay people, but probably it was not so. For the bishop, the numerous members of the chapter, the abbots of neighbouring monasteries and the priests of the diocese must have contributed to the decoration of the cathedral. It may well be that the many windows without signatures were offered by men of the church who did not care to be commemorated.

These donor images are extremely interesting : they show us all the guild members at work. The money changers weigh coins in their scales ; the furriers show a prospective buyer an ermine coat, the sculptors sketch out sculptures in their niches and stop a moment to drain a goblet of wine, the innkeepers serve the travellers sitting

Pages 158 and 159 :

125. Blue Virgin window :
"Notre-Dame de la Belle Verrière"

126. Saint James window.

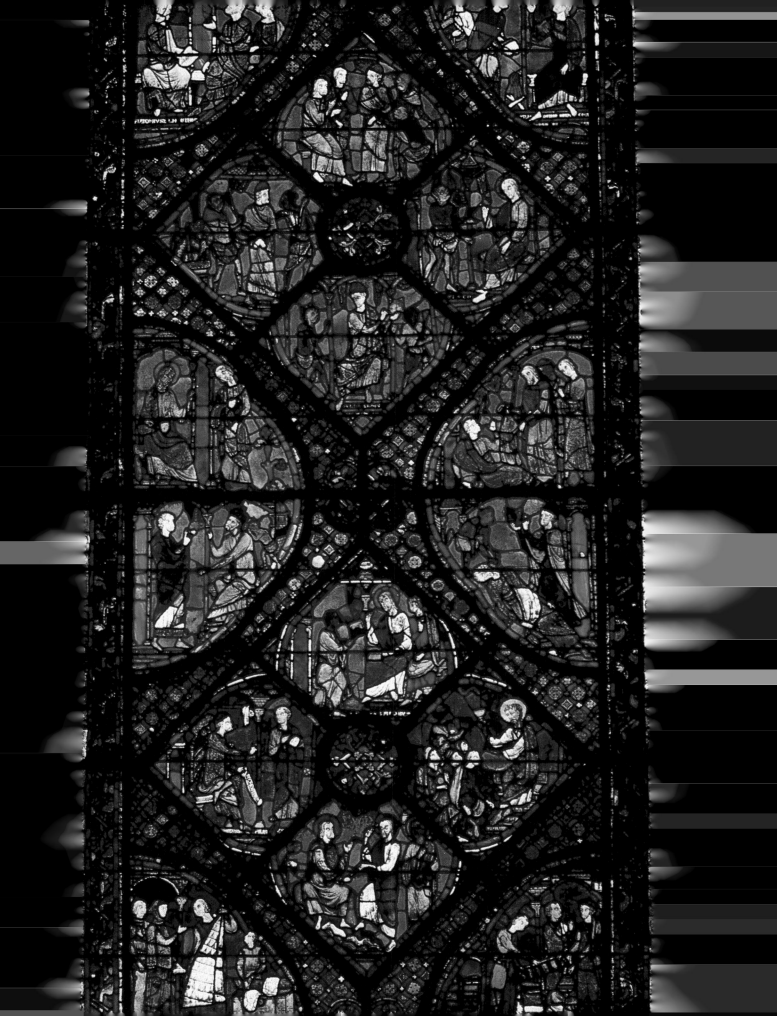

at the inn door, half naked bakers carry baskets of little rolls hot from the oven, the smiths stir up the fire, hammer the iron on the anvil, and shoe the horse penned in his wooden frame. These everyday scenes mingle with the lives of the saints; they seem not at all out of place, since, according to the wise, man's labour works for his redemption. One can even see in the ambulatory a window exclusively devoted to the monthly labours of the peasant, scenes which harmonise with the signs of the zodiac; an image of Christ looks down upon man's eternal travail and brings him hope.

The chivalric orders of France form another category of donors. Here are found the noblest names of the lands around Chartres, of the Ile-de-France and the neighbouring regions, names redolent of history. They may be recognised by their coats of arms rather than by inscriptions. Here are the four eaglets quartering the cross of gules of the Montmorency family, so the stained glass predates 1214, when Philippe Auguste authorised Mathieu de Montmorency to add to the original four eaglets twelve new ones, to commemorate the twelve standards he captured in battle. Here is the lion argent, rearing on the field of gules of the Monfort family. The knight who bears these proud arms must be the famous Simon de Monfort, who headed the crusade against the Albigeois, and who was killed before the walls of Toulouse in 1218. This shield with the three roundels in gules on a field of or belongs to the Courtenay family; a Courtenay was an emperor of Byzantium. The argent cross established on an azure field denotes the Clement family, Lords of Metz in Gatinais, which produced three marshals of France. A Clement was killed at the siege of Saint-Jean-d'Acre, another fought most bravely at Bouvines, and was celebrated by the poet Guillaume le Breton, a third accompanied Saint Louis to Egypt with distinction. A stained glass window of epic grandeur celebrates one of these Clements; the knight standing clad in the fine armour of the thirteenth century, with his coat of arms emblazoned on his tunic, receives a red banner with five points from the hand of Saint Denis; this is no less than the oriflamme, the flag of France. Is this the hero of Bouvines, who died in 1214, or is it rather Jean Clement, his son, who was also Marshal of France from 1225 onwards? The second hypothesis accords better with the setting of the window, which is at the end of the transept, that is to say the most recent part of the cathedral.

There are still nobler figures here. Several windows of the northern arm of transept were given by a prince of royal blood, Philippe, Count of Boulogne, and by his wife Mahaut. Philippe of Boulogne, son of Philippe Auguste and of Agnes de Meranie bears the lilies or on an azure field.

Pierre Mauclerc, donor of the southern rose window and its lancets, was himself a prince of the House of France, for he was the great grandson of Louis le Gros. His pride made him a rebel. He opposed Blanche of Castile and her infant son. When Saint Louis became a king, he pardoned him. Surprisingly, Mauclerc's splendid rose window faces the no less magnificent rose window offered by Blanche de Castile, but in the church of the Virgin, the rivals forgot their quarrels.

Many stained glass windows of the choir were donated, some by the king of France, some by the king and queen of Castile: but the ignorant canons of the eighteenth century who cannot have looked closely at such treasures had them replaced by transparent glass. A very old description and some drawings by Gaignières give us some idea of them. Two windows recounted episodes in the martyrdom of Saint Denis, protector of the royal family, and a king of France, recognisable by the innumerable "fleurs de lis" on his coat of arms, was to be seen kneeling at the base of the two windows. Was it Philippe Auguste who died in 1223 or his son Louis VIII? It is difficult to decide[6]. The window was given by the king of Castile, as capital letters spell out REX CASTELLE, and it was dedicated to Saint James of Compostella, the great saint of Spain. There is every reason to believe that this king of Castile was Saint Ferdinand, the cousin of Saint Louis, and the conqueror of the Moors. As he reigned from 1217 to 1252, it must have been only a few years after his coronation that he gave the Saint James window to the cathedral. The tower of Castile may also be seen here, but not the lion of Leon, which proves that the window dates from before 1230 at least, at which date

127. Charlemagne window.

6. Canon Delaporte, *op. cit.* 476 opts for Louis VIII, because his image on horseback which is preserved in the rose window above the destroyed lancet does not wear a crown, unlike the neighbouring image of the king of Castile. The lancet would have been donated, in this case, by the future Louis VIII during the lifetime of his father, Philippe Auguste. It is still rather peculiar, however, that it is not the king of France himself, but the heir apparent who is in the place of honour.

Ferdinand, king of Castile also became king of Leon. Happily the stained glass has not disappeared completely, for in the rose window, an equestrian figure of Saint Ferdinand survives. One of the destroyed rose windows depicting the martyrdom of Saint Denis has likewise preserved for us an image of the king of France on horseback. These two figures are magnificent, and almost identical ones may be found in the surviving rose windows donated by high ranking barons. Grasping their standards, with their shields on their arms and their faces hidden by the formal and clean design of thirteenth century helmets, their tunics over coats of gilded mail, they are set against a brilliant background, like a vision of ancient chivalry. Whatever the privileges of these knights, they were always ready to earn them in the garb of the soldier.

The windows : subject matter

We must ask to what extent the clergy of Chartres was able to impose an overall plan on so many donors. An attempt was made in some parts of the cathedral. The five windows rising above the choir, which would hold the gaze of the faithful as they made their way towards the altar, do form a poem in honour of the Virgin. The guilds which donated them, the furriers, bakers, butchers and shoemakers, had in this instance to comply with the instruction of the clergy. In the main axis of the chuch, at the top of a window showing the Annunciation and Visitation, the Virgin appears carrying the Child on her knees : her tall crown, her huge eyes and her solemn gravity bestow on her a supernatural grandeur. Her depiction was archaic, in keeping with the sculpted Virgin on the Portail Royal and that of the Blue Virgin window, "Notre-Dame de la Belle Verrière". Truly Our Lady of Chartres, the same image is found repeatedly in the rose windows and elsewhere[7]. The prophets who announced her coming fill the neighbouring windows : Daniel, Ezekiel, David, Aaron, Moses, Isaiah. Moses stands before the burning bush, symbol of his virginity, and Isaiah carries the rod of Jesse, image of his nobility. At the Virgin's side, an angel wafts incense upon her ; the wings raised and lowered describe a beautiful arabesque. These five windows are evidently the creation of a single thought.

The great rose windows also form a coherent, well ordered whole. The southern rose window, donated by Pierre Mauclerc, celebrates Christ in eternity : his throne is at the centre of this great disc of colour and light. Around him shine the angels in their radiance, the symbolic beasts, and finally the twenty-four Elders of the Apocalypse carrying golden cups and zithers and chanting songs of celebration in praise of the Eternal. The lancets beneath them however bring us down from heaven to earth : they remind us that the coming of Christ triumphant was spoken of in the Old Testament as well as told in the New, and that a profound harmony exists between the two books. For this reason the four major prophets, Isaiah, Daniel, Ezekiel and Jeremiah are portrayed carrying the four Apostles on their shoulders : Matthew, John, Mark and Luke. Thus the Apostles found their message prefigured in the prophets, but could see higher and further than they could. These solemn figures retain a nobility despite the strangeness of their pose. It is very unlikely that the daring symbolism of these groups was conceived by a theologian from Chartres. In the church of San Sebastiano in Pallara in Rome, I have noticed the remains of a fresco from the end of the tenth century where prophets bearing the Apostles on their backs may still be traced. The idea is identical, and presumes the existence of an original prototype which provided the inspiration for the figures at both Chartres and Rome[8].

The northern rose window, given by Blanche of Castile and Saint-Louis is similarly well planned as a whole. It is a celebration of both the Virgin and her Son. The Mother of God, bearing the Child on her knees takes up the centre ; doves and angels form a first circle around her. The kings of Judah, her ancestors, placed in square medallions form a second circle and the twelve minor prophets form a third. Beneath the rose window, tall, solemn standing figures fill the lancet windows : all prophesy the coming of Christ and his Mother. In the centre, Saint Anne, whose relics were the pride of Chartres, bears the infant Virgin in her arms, at her side, Melchisedeck holds the bread

128. Parable of the Prodigal Son. He is seen with two courtesans playing dice, and then stripped of his possessions, talking to a woman who chases him away with a cudgel.

Pages 164 and 165 :

129. Saint Cheron window.

130. Saint Eustace window.

7. The statue of Notre-Dame-sous-Terre, now destroyed, was also of the same type.
8. *Revue des Deux Mondes. Études sur les églises de Rome. L'Empereur Otton III à Rome et les églises du Xe siècle*, 1937. This chapter may be found reprinted in my publication : *Rome et ses vieilles Églises*, 1942, p. 157.

and the wine, symbols of the Eucharist, Aaron bears the flowering branch, symbol of virgin motherhood, David predicts the Passion, and Solomon the Adoration of the Magi. Beneath their feet are those who violated the divine law : Nebuchadnezzar and Jereboam adoring idols, Saul stabbing himself with his sword and the Pharoah plunging into the waves in pursuit of the children of God. Time has given some of these figures a grandiose and terrible appearance. The brown faces of Aaron and Melchisedeck have become black, against which the whites of their eyes stare in sombre contrast. Saint Anne herself seems like an Indian princess. Yet the blue of the rose window, that beautiful blue of the arms of France, illuminates and softens the whole.

The clergy of Chartres sometimes tried to unite the gifts of various donors in this way, within a previously planned structure. Normally, however, they did not attempt this, feeling that they should respect an individual's devotion to a particular saint. This is why there are, for example, five windows consecrated to Saint Nicholas and four to Saint Martin. But it is above all Our Lady of Chartres, Notre-Dame, whom men wished to honour, and there are over twenty stained glass or rose windows all dedicated to her. Sometimes the artist has recounted certain episodes in the story of her life ; sometimes he has represented her alone with her Son. Very probably some of these works were created as the result of a vow : hence the church found itself obliged to respect the donor's promise. For Chartres cathedral is above all a pilgrimage church, and most of its sumptuous stained glass windows are *ex-voto* offerings. Nor was Notre-Dame the sole object of faithful devotion : the pilgrim who had been as far as Saint James of Compostella would give an image of this Spanish Apostle[9], and one who had only reached Conques in the mountains of Rouergue would give an image of Saint Foy[10].

We can sometimes guess the reasons which governed the donors' choice. The tradesmen's guilds which began to assume a definite form at the beginning of the thirteenth century might offer the image or the legend of their patron saint, or of a saintly character whose life in some respect evoked their sympathy. Thus the grocers donated the story of Saint Nicholas, who remained the patron of their guild for many centuries : the masons and the stoneworkers offered that of Saint Sylvester, the great church builder[11] ; the carpenters the story of Noah, builder of the ark, or Saint Julian whose roof beam was a shelter for travellers. But why did the furriers choose Saint Eustace, and the money changers Saint Peter ? No reason can be discerned. One feels that the saints who protected the guilds of craftsmen were not as clearly defined by tradition as they were later. Certain choices are surprising, and there is evidence that the craftsmen, wishing to donate a window would sometimes leave the choice to the learning of the clergy ; otherwise how could the blacksmiths have chosen the subject of the Redemption window themselves with its involved symbolism, or the shoemakers selected their parable of the Good Samaritan together with its profound theological commentary ?

Individuals would pay homage to the saint whose name they bore : Marguerite de Lèves' gift was the legend of Saint Marguerite ; but the barons would eagerly offer the legend of a military saint that they considered to be their patron in spirit : a Courtenay and a de Beaumont, each man a soldier, chose Saint George and Saint Eustache respectively. There is every reason to believe that the handsome Saint George apparelled as a Byzantine warrior in an upper storey window in the nave was donated by a knight who hat not forgotten that Saint George appeared in the Orient at the head of the crusaders at the siege of Antioch. It was natural for the king of France to donate Saint Denis, protector of the French monarchy, and for the king of Castile to give Saint James, the "Matamoro", or slayer of the Moors. In most cases, however, we have to admit that the reasons for the donors' choices remain unknown : a vow made during battle, devotion to a saint in a particular family, a relic preserved in a place of prayer at home, or even in a sword-pommel — these may be explanations.

The relics which enriched the cathedral also had their own kind of influence. The stained glass window dedicated to Saint Thomas à Becket of Canterbury in one of the

9. One of the high nave windows shows Saint James with pilgrims beneath his feet who have the famous scallop shells from Compostella on their bread baskets. One of the choir windows which simply shows pilgrims with shells on their baskets doubtless represents a brotherhood of Saint James with their leader, Robert de Bérou, the donor of the window.
10. Nave window.
11. Saint Sylvester was also the patron saint of masons in Rome.

radiating chapels is an example of this. When the bishop was assassinated in his cathedral, his blood spurted on to one of the clergy in his entourage, John of Salisbury, who later became bishop of Chartres. He brought a few drops of the martyr's blood in a reliquary to the cathedral, and thus the cult of the saintly English prelate was established at Chartres, as the stained glass window proves.

The dedications to various saints in the chapels radiating from the choir were changed over the centuries, but thanks to *Parthénie,* the ancient book by Sebastian Rouillard, we know the original names. These names corresponded to the various relics enshrined in the altars, as was customary in the Middle Ages. Hence the stained glass windows of several of these chapels portray the saints to whom they were originally dedicated, corresponding to such relics. So it is that in the chapel of Saint Julian a window tells his dramatic story. In the chapel of Saint-Étienne and the Martyrs, the central window is dedicated to the story of Saint Stephen and the neighbouring windows to those of Saint Potentien, Saint Savinien, Saint Chéron and Saint Pantaléon, all martyrs, and finally to the legend of an unknown female saint, also martyred. The central chapel of the ambulatory is dedicated to the apostles. Thus, the window in the middle retraces the story of the calling of the Apostles, and those scenes from the gospel where Christ addresses the entire apostolic gathering, while the stained glass in the other windows tells the legends of Saint Peter, Saint Paul, Saint Simon and Saint Jude following the apocryphal acts attributed to them.

If the canons could not impose the unity they would have liked upon the stained glass windows, as they did for the statuary, it seems nonetheless that for the most part they gave very precise instructions to the artists. They made sure that they understood the character of the saints who were to be depicted ; they taught them the identities of Saint Foy, Saint Mary the Egyptian, Saint Giles, Saint Laumer : hence the nobility and the perfectly apt portrayal of those great figures in the nave windows. As for the narrative stained glass in small sections, the general lines of development and often even the details were fixed in advance by the clerics. There are symbolic windows where everything has a proper meaning and nothing could be left to individual fancy. The legends of the saints left a great deal more liberty to the artist, and his imagination could often be given free rein in this area : nevertheless, the sequence of episodes had to be determined in advance. The reading books in the choir stalls, the lectionaries, a few of which are still preserved at Chartres, normally provided the stories suggested to the master stained-glass maker. The legends of Saint Nicholas or Saint Martin were translated for him, the miraculous life of Saint Eustace, or the battles of the Apostles, Saint Simon and Saint Jude with the magicians of the Orient. Most of the stories which Jacques de Voragine was later to collect in his book *La Légende dorée,* were to be found in the cathedral lectionaries. On certain days members of the clergy would probably explain the subjects to the pilgrims who looked at these windows.

All these legends were full of the wonders which enchanted the men of medieval times ; having all the interest of stories, they had quite another significance, in showing God continually present in his creation. The saints, thanks to whom faith and charity triumph over the earth, are his instruments. Their example teaches that there is only one force in this world, that of the soul which commands nature and can even vanquish death. In this way these windows, where almost all is miraculous, strengthened faith by awakening the spirit, and gave birth to hope in the hearts of men.

Other stained glass windows at Chartres

Here a few examples must serve to give an idea of the innumerable subjects the windows offered for contemplation and worship. Let us look first of all at a « dogmatic » window which illustrates the most profound significance of the divine Word[12]. It portrays the story of the Good Samaritan, perhaps the most touching of the parables in the Gospel. The learned men of the Middle Ages saw it, as we do, as a lesson of charity, but beyond this they perceived further secrets. The window reveals these for us. Its composition is extremely unusual. The lower part is entirely devoted to the Gospel story : one sees the traveller leaving Jerusalem ; next, attacked and assaulted by

12. Right side aisle, third window counting from the back of the church.

thieves, with his tunic and all his belongings stolen from him. He lies naked, half dead ; the priest and the Levite pass by on the other side, throw him a backward glance and move on with indifference. The Good Samaritan, however, whom the artist portrays with the countenance of Christ, then arrives, stops, binds the wounds of the injured man, puts him on his horse and leads him to an inn ; and before he leaves visits the sick man in his room. All is perfectly clear up to this point, but the following episodes in the window are disconcerting : the creation of Adam and Eve, their sin, their expulsion from earthly Paradise, their condemnation to perpetual labour and finally the murder of Abel. The juxtaposition is by no means accidental : the second part is a commentary on the first. According to all medieval scholarship, the story of the traveller is decidedly that of humanity as a whole[13]. The traveller is man : he is attacked by a group of thieves, that is to say by all the sins together, who fall upon him and take away his tunic, symbol of his immortality. Such was Adam, condemned, after his sin, along with his descendants to labour and to death. The priest and the Levite represent the Law of Moses and the Old Testament incapable of the salvation of a sick humanity. The Good Samaritan is Christ himself, who binds the wounds that Moses was unable to heal and who leads man into an inn, in other words into the Church. This view explains why the history of the Fall has its place in the parable and why the figure of Christ dominates the whole composition[14]. It is obvious that the shoemaker's guild which made this gift to the cathedral left the task of designing the window to the clergy.

Not very far from this window[15] is another worth our attention, despite the fact that only its lower part has been preserved. Represented here, we see two heavy carts with four wheels apiece, one loaded with bursting sacks, one with a huge barrel. Not horses but men are harnessed to them, and a banner unfurls above their heads. These wagons are heading towards a statue of the Virgin surrounded by pilgrims at prayer. Here, the sources for these images are undoubtedly the episodes recounted in the *Livre de Miracles de Notre-Dame de Chartres*. We recognise the peasants from the villages in the Beauce region, harnessing themselves to wagons and coming to bring wheat, wine, stones and lime to the workers who were rebuilding the cathedral after the old one burnt down in 1194. The statue worshipped by pilgrims is Notre-Dame de Chartres, and above her the Virgin sits looking down from her throne in the sky. So this is a rare instance of the commemoration of an almost contemporary event, which perhaps the artist himself witnessed. One window shows clearly how the lives of the saints appeared to medieval man. It is at the entrance to the northern side-aisle to the Church and is consecrated to Saint Germain of Auxerre[16]. This noble Gallo-Roman, having married and spent his youth as a man of the world revealed the noblest spiritual qualities once he became a bishop. His charity and his fervour marked him as one of the most attractive figures of the fifth century. In this window he appears solely as a miracle-worker. The moment he was anointed bishop, the power of his prayer allowed him to recognise a criminal previously undiscovered. The devil, troubled by Saint Germain's prestige, decided to engage in a battle with him and spread a contagious disease throughout Auxerre. The bishop blessed the sick with oil, and healed them. He was called to Great Britain, to combat the increasing success of the Pelagian heresy. The devil, ever bent on his destruction, unleashed the winds and attempted to sink the boat which was carrying him ; Saint Germain was aroused from sleep, and lifting a hand he stilled the tempest. Seeing the heresy vanquished, the devil resolved to be finished with his enemy and set fire to the town where the bishop had stopped for the night ; the houses burned, but the fire halted in front of where Saint Germain was sleeping. Here he is again, now setting off for Italy with his retinue at the first stage of the journey, a thief makes off with his horse. Saint Germain shows not the slightest anxiety, for he knows what will happen in advance. The thief, wandering all night without being able to find his path, which seems to escape him, is finally constrained to lead the horse back to its owner, and the good bishop, welcoming him, gives him absolution and alms. At the top of the window, Saint Germain is stretched out on his death bed at Ravenna, and angels are carrying his soul to the heavens. Thus in this window, guided by the donor,

Pages 172 and 173 :

134. Saint Giles window.

135. Saint George window.

13. This is confirmed in the *Glose ordinaire* in Lucam X, and in Honorius d'Autun, *Spec. Ecclesiae, Domin. XIII post Pentecost.*
14. The Good Samaritain windows at Sens and Bourges cathedrals are very much more complete than at Chartres.
15. Right side aisle, sixth window.
16. The interpretation of this window remained a mystery until all its elements were fully explained in Canon Delaporte's publication, *op. cit.*, pp. 370 ff. The work took the Chartres Lectionary as its source.

Archdeacon Chardonel, the artist has celebrated the purely supernatural powers of the saintly bishop. At the time, people believed that God's true servants could be recognised through miracles. These were the men on earth to whom he sometimes assigned something of his heavenly powers.

The window of Saint Germain of Auxerre is simply a series of miracles ; Saint Julian the Hospitaller's window tells a most dramatic story[17]. This extraordinary narrative whose source remains unknown begins in the manner of an epic of chivalry. Julian is taken by his parents to a knight who welcomes him and takes him into his service. The young man serves at table and demonstrates so many oustanding qualities, that his master, presenting him with a sceptre, creates him master of several fiefs. A faithful vassal, Julian is beside his lord when the latter is about to die ; he is seen holding his suzerain's head, so that the last sacrament might be received. Then Julian's life unfurls in the manner of a knight of the Round Table ; just married, he sets off in search of adventure. He sleeps in a tent ; he presents himself with his squire at the foot of some enchanted castle with its fluttering banner, and holds a dialogue with the guardian of the tower ; he meets enemy knights and puts them to flight. Finally, having adventured the length and breadth of the world, he arrives on horseback at his manor gate. He goes into his wife's bedchamber, to waken her and give himself the pleasure of surprising her, but in the half light he makes out two heads on the pillow. Without a moment's hesitation, he draws his sword and kills the man and the woman without even taking the time to look at them. While he wipes his bloody sword, his wife, returning from an early morning mass, recounts in tears how Julian's father and mother had come to the castle the previous evening, and how she had given them her room in honour of their visit. Julian learns with horror that he has unwittingly killed his parents, and henceforth he has no thought but to expiate his crime. Having buried his victims and mourned for them, he leaves his castle, accompanied by his wife, who has resolved to share in his penitence. He sets himself up beside a river with a fast-flowing current, to take travellers in his boat to the opposite bank. He builds them a house for shelter, where we see him welcoming them and washing their feet. One night he hears a passer-by calling him ; immediately he takes the man on to his boat and while his wife holds a flaming torch ferries him to the other side. This traveller was none other than Christ himself, come back to earth to reward his servants. That very night, in fact, the angels carried Julian's soul to the heavens, together with that of his wife. This story was much loved in the Middle Ages for its moving and dramatic qualities, but also because of its ending, which teaches the virtue of expiation. The carpenters who donated the window learnt as they deciphered its message, that man must never despair and that penitence restores baptismal innoncence to the soul[18].

One unusual window praises not saintliness but heroism. It portrays not the history but the legend of Charlemagne[19]. It is a work of pure poetry, based on three different narratives in which figures the great Emperor as hero. The first part of the window, at the base, illustrates the fabulous account of the *Voyage de Charlemagne en Orient.* In a dream, the emperor of Byzantium sees a magnificent knight dressed in his own armour, and an angel tells him that this stranger will soon take possession of Jesuralem. This mysterious knight is none other than Charlemagne, who, in fact, delivers Christ's tomb from the infidel, and returns to France via Byzantium. To thank him, the oriental emperor gives him relics of the Passion which Charlemagne placed in the church at Aix-la-Chapelle. Now it is the turn of the *Chronique de Turpin* to inspire the artist. One night, Charlemagne dreams of Saint James the Apostle. Saint James invites him to follow the direction of the Milky Way and lead his army into Spain. Charlemagne obeys him and takes possession of Pamplona. Soon he will join battle with Aygoland, prince of the infidels, and during the night, the lances of those Christian knights who must die on the morrow burst into flower. Roland in particular distinguishes himself during this battle, and he may be seen triumphant in single combat with the giant Feragut. Charlemagne returns victorious to France, but during the passage through the mountains, Roland is ambushed with the rear guard. Having fought all day

17. This legend does not appear in the Chartres Lectionary, its source is elsewhere. The window is situated in the first small radiating chapel to the north.
18. The Chartres window noticeably omits the famous episode where a deer prophesies Julian's crime in advance to the Saint. This episode appears later in the *Legende dorée,* but the oldest versions of the story seem to have been unfamiliar with it.
19. Ambulatory : small chapel to the left of the central chapel.

long, gashed all over with wounds, at the end of his strength, and feeling the approach of death, he wants to shatter Durandal, his sword, but the blade cleaves the rock without breaking. He resolves finally to sound his horn and alert Charlemagne, then falling back, he collapses, exhausted, and awaits death. Baudoin, who wanted to bring a little water to him in his helmet, looks in vain for a spring, and Charlemagne soon learns of the hero's death from Baudoin himself. A last panel is inspired by the legend of Saint Giles. While the hermit saint was celebrating mass in front of Charlemagne, an angel brings a scroll down from the sky, inscribed with the name of the sin the emperor dared not avow during confession.

In this window, Charlemagne and Roland are represented with halos : Charlemagne had, in fact, been consecrated in the twelfth century by an antipope and Roland is often styled *Sanctus* in the older Passionals. This window of Chartres is the fragment of an epic, inspired with the excitement of the crusades. This fine window was particular in that its lower part was an imitation of a window from Saint-Denis, now destroyed, whose appearance has been preserved for us in Montfaucon's drawing[20]. Here were to be seen the various episodes of Charlemagne's voyages in the East. Seventy years old, the works inspired by Suger kept all of their prestige[21]. It would be pleasant to describe all those windows which were like a great picture book for the fascinated pilgrims. In the story of Noah, we see the ark raised up by the waves of the Flood, and among the animals saved by the patriarch, beside the horse and the elephant, are the winged griffon with the eagle's beak ; the story of Joseph, son of Jacob, with the desert camels passing by ; the parable of the Prodigal Son, where exotic women crown the young man with a garland of flowers ; the miracles of Saint John the Evangelist, changing pebbles into precious stones and precious stones into pebbles ; the travels of Saint Thomas who was ordered by king Gondoforus to build a palace for him in India ; the apostolate of Saint Madeleine, landing on the coast of Provence ; the adventures of Saint Eustace, losing his wife and sons and then finding them again, and then dying with his family inside the bronze bull.

The three great windows of the façade introduce us to the art of the twelfth century in all its perfection. But the changes that lead from these to the early thirteenth century windows of the nave and the side aisles are not clearly defined. We cannot understand the development fully, as all the windows donated to the ancient cathedral of Chartres during the second part of the twelfth century are missing, as are those of the choir and the nave of Notre-Dame de Paris which date from the same period.

The first thirteenth century windows that appeared at Chartres in about 1205 or 1210 show a number of technical innovations. The armature of the window into which the glass panels were inserted had changed. Instead of being constructed on the former model — iron bars intersecting at right angles and framing squares or rectangles — the armature was now an elaborate network of circles, semi-circles, trefoils and quatrefoils. The skillfully wrought iron was already a veritable work of art before the glass itself was inserted. Each scene enclosed within this framework was separated from the others and became perfectly identified. In the high windows stand those huge figures whose dimensions are so perfectly suited to their position. Did this confident innovation originate at Chartres ? One would think so, but in fact, before the Revolution, tall figures dating from the twelfth century filled the windows of the choir at Notre-Dame de Paris[22].

At Chartres, if one looks carefully at the scenes represented in the narrative windows of the side aisles, one is struck by the new originality of the design. In the twelfth century, drapery clung so closely to the limbs that their outlines could be perceived ; in the thirteenth century, the tendency was for more ample flowing robes in which the body was more comfortable. The artists, abandoning the secular traditions

The art of the stained glass makers

20. *Monum. de la monarchie française*, vol. I, p. 227, pl. XXII.
21. Other borrowings from Saint Denis may be found at Chartres in the Passion window which shows Old Testament figures who were symbolic precursors of event. See on this point *L'art religieux du XIIᵉ siècle en France*, pp. 160 ff.
22. This is according to the painter Levieil, who was responsible for the removal of these windows in the eighteenth century.

bequeathed by Byzantine art, made an effort towards a greater realism and to reproducing what they saw. At the same period, gestures more carefully observed made the relationships between the figures themselves more natural.

This was remarkable progress ; nevertheless one is forced to recognise that the purely decorative portion of the window is not always treated with the patience and perfect craftsmanship of the previous century. The magnificent decorative borders of the twelfth century become narrower, the beautiful stylised foliage that filled in the gaps between the medallions is replaced by imbrications and soon by a simple red trellis overlay on a blue background. The need for substantial output within a limited period sometimes forced the master glaziers to sacrifice the richness of decoration. But there still is stained glass in the side aisles and the high windows of the nave whose decoration is almost as perfect as before : the fine window dedicated to Saint Eustace is numbered among these. At no other period could a more sumptuous Saint James be imagined than the one we see in one of the nave windows : thrown over his tunic is a blue mantle sewn with innumerable silver scallops, which give the garments of this Apostle-pilgrim the magnificence of a huge coat-of-arms.

The artists never lost the intensity of their sense of colour. The stained glass windows of Chartres form a dazzling ensemble, equalled by no other cathedral. The tones are few — the blue, the red, a little yellow and green, a few touches of white, and sometimes a brown tending towards deep purple ; their exquisite relationships create a magical harmony. All these colours brighten with brilliant skies, and become subdued when the sky is overcast. They fill the cathedral with an unreal light, constantly changing with the hours of the day and the passing clouds. Brilliant or subdued, they open up a world of dreams. How many hearts have been uplifted by their distant reflection of the light "which the eye of man hath not seen" ! The frescoes of our Romanesque churches with their muted colours had their beauty, but were restrained to earth, while the stained glass windows seem to want to transport us far from its realms.

At the beginning of the thirteenth century, Chartres was the great school for painting on glass. The windows at Bourges, and certain of those at Tours, Le Mans, Rouen and Canterbury bear striking resemblances to those at Chartres. In fact, one of the windows at Rouen, that of Saint Julian the Hospitaller, was signed by a stained glass artist from Chartres : *"Clemens vitrarius Carnotensis"*.

Such was the vast influence of this illustrious church of Chartres, which drew pilgrims from all over northern France. For nearly a century, from about 1145-1235, generations of architects, sculptors and masters of stained glass came to seek their inspiration there.

136. Grisaille window, fourteenth century : Canon Thierry.

177

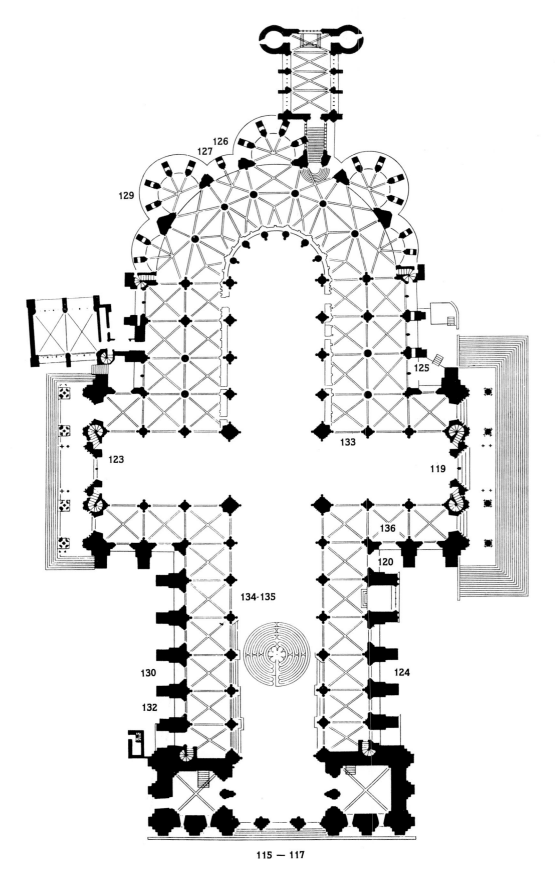

126
127
129
125
133
123
119
136
120
134-135
130
124
132
115 — 117

The numbers refer to reproductions
of stained glass windows
and indicate their location
in the cathedral

20 m

138. The Prodigal Son herding swine.

6. Chartres cathedral after the thirteenth century

Today's visitors come to Chartres to admire the architecture of the twelfth and thirteenth centuries, the truly great centuries of the Middle Ages. Generally they care very little for the architectural additions after 1260, the date when the cathedral was consecrated. However, it would be unjust not to mention these additions briefly, for some of them are very beautiful, and all testify to the unfailing love inspired by the Virgin of Chartres.

During the first years of the fourteenth century the gables of the façade and their statues were completed. The great work achieved, the people of Chartres, happy to see the cathedral finally freed of its winches, cranes and scaffolding, rejoiced. But the rich and generous chapter, as if tormented by an unceasing desire to beautify their church, added a chapter house to the apse in 1335, which was surmounted by a holy chapel of sorts, shortly afterwards in 1344. It was dedicated to Saint Piat, whose long forgotten relics had been rediscovered a few years before. The covered staircase connecting the

Saint Piat chapel turned the latter into an annexe. Hugues d'Ivry, and ... vry, probably father and son, were in charge of the works. While the ... quite bare, the interior is enriched by elegantly designed mullioned windows ... ned glass, some of which can still be seen.

... e fifteenth century, though ravaged by foreign and civil wars, still brought ... ut changes at Chartres. The Vendôme chapel, built between two buttresses of the ... outhern side aisles, was begun in 1417, two years after the battle of Agincourt. In 1421, when the King of England, Henry V, established an English garrison at Chartres, the decoration was probably not completely finished. As Chartres cathedral kept its initial ground-plan intact throughout the church, this chapel is the only one to open on to the side aisles. The chapel was built as the result of a vow made by Louis de Bourbon, Count of Vendôme, while he was the prisoner of his brother Jacques, Count of La Marche. Count Louis de Vendôme, who later fought by the side of Joan of Arc, was a descendant of Saint Louis and was one of the ancestors of Henry IV. He was clearly of a generous nature, for he forgave his brother who had caused him so much trouble. He wanted their reconciliation to be inscribed in the stained glass windows of his chapel. Thus, in this beautiful window there are four kneeling couples protected by saints beneath the Coronation of the Virgin. Their shields which are held by angels make these large figures recognisable ; the father and mother of Louis de Vendôme ; his sister accompanied by her husband, a Lusignan, who is decorated with two kingships ; the imaginary kingship of Jerusalem and the real kingship of Cyprus ; his brother, Jacques de la Marche, his enemy of yesteryear, and his wife, the second Jeanne of Naples, who does not seem to have been any more virtuous than the first. Jacques de la Marche, disillusioned and weary of his lamentable century, took Franciscan orders, and it is in a monk's habit that he is represented as a statue on the chapel's exterior. Finally, in the last light, Louis de Vendôme himself appears with his wife Blanche de Roucy. This very interesting window has been badly affected by time and has had to be restored in parts ; the modern portions are numerous. The remaining lights, however, make it a fine work of the fifteenth century. Its pale yellows and attenuated blues, and the beautiful pinnacles of its architecture, where the white is picked out in gold, relate it to the admirable stained glass at Bourges cathedral, designed in the time of the Duc de Berry.

The sixteenth century begins at Chartres with a masterpiece. In 1506 a fire started by lightning destroyed the lead-covered wooden spire, which rose above the old southern tower of the façade. The chapter decided to replace it with a stone spire, and summoned a mason from Vendôme named Jean Texier, known as Jean de Beauce, to build it. This mason, one of the greatest architects of the end of the Middle Ages, was given a daily contract and was paid seven sous and six deniers per day, scarcely twice the rate of his own labourers. His spire is the finest ever built in the sixteenth century.

Above the twelfth century tower, he constructed a square storey pierced with a huge window, to which he added two octagonal stages to serve as the base of the spire. These are adorned with statues of the apostles and held up by small flying buttresses with elegantly designed curves and counter-curves. Pinnacles flowered everywhere, trefoils, skewbacks, mullions — and all seemed delicate as lace. The spire, covered with graciously overlapping tiles which resemble a heraldic decor, soars above this aerial crown.

Framing the façade with their unequal height, these two spires represent the beginning and the end of the architecture of the Middle Ages : on the one hand, just simplicity and grandeur ; on the other, all the delicacy and the richness of an art refined and perfected by four centuries of masterpieces. Gothic art, whose death was imminent, culminated triumphantly at Chartres.

In 1513, when Jean de Beauce had just finished his spire, the chapter asked him to screen off the choir with a stone wall. In the thirteenth century the choir had been separated from the nave by a rood screen, upon which the life of Christ was represented. (The canons of the eighteenth century, judging it unstable, had it demolished without a scruple in 1763.) Today, only a few charming bas-reliefs representing the Annunciation, the Nativity, the Annunciation to the Shepherds and the sleep of the Magi, remain preserved in the crypt. Their beauty makes the destruction of this rood screen quite deplorable. These bas-reliefs, which do not appear to be all by the same hand, seem to date from before the middle of the thirteenth century.

139. Jean de Beauce's spire.   181

In 1514, when Jean de Beauce was beginning his work, it became necessary to screen off the choir on the ambulatory side ; it had already been closed on the nave side by the rood screen. With the choir screen he designed, the architect remained faithful to earlier Gothic architecture. It had large open spaces for statues and was crowned with a dazzingly elaborate arrangement of pinnacles ; the lower parts were lined with blind arches, and the buttresses were laden with canopies harbouring statuettes. When he created his spire Jean de Beauce's imagination was restrained by the laws of architecture. Here it was given free rein. Beginning the construction of the wall on either side at the same time, he first sealed off the two primary northern and southern arcades. This is the most perfect part of his work. He continued it a little later, and when he died in 1529, it was not completely finished. It is strange that this champion of Gothic art was touched by the graces of the classical Renaissance. In 1520, the chapter commissioned him to build a room for a clock at the base of the tower which bore his spire. He showed that he, too, was aware of the new ornamental grammar in its decoration : the clock face was flanked with classical pilasters, the cornice was decorated with dentils and egg-and-tongue moulding, and the buttresses were topped by candelabras in a classical style. This also explains the proliferation of classical motifs on the most recent parts of the choir screen : beautiful Florentine or Lombardian arabesques, medallions of the Caesars and classical scenes from Italian plaques. This marriage of two styles is full of charm and the architecture of the reigns of Louis XII and of François I was marked by the same graceful union.

It was to take two centuries to fill the setting Jean de Beauce prepared with sculpture. The earliest and most attractive of those sculptors who worked on this project was Jean Soulas, from Paris. Between 1519 and 1525, in the first four bays of the south, he told the story of Saint Anne and Saint Joachim, followed by the Nativity of the Virgin. These simple statues with their jovial expressions stand out from their background and are posed like the figures of a Mystery play. In the purest French tradition, these scenes have no grandeur, but gentle, intimate charm. The costumes are contemporary : the shepherds have linen cross-garters, their sheep shears hang from their belts ; the serving girls, wearing coifs that hide their hair, hurry to and fro with pewter mugs in their hands.

After 1525 Jean Soulas told the story of the Virgin from the Presentation at the Temple to the Adoration of the Magi. This continued his charming style of sculpture. Here is the matron with a bunch of keys at her belt, and the servant girl with a little basket on her arm ; here we see the Virgin sewing while Saint Joseph sleeps, and receiving the Wise Men, with her psalter and her rosary beside the Christ child on her lap[1].

In 1542 however, everything changed suddenly, with the appearance of François Marchand. This is the reign of the School of Fontainebleau. The Roman soldiers of triumphal bas-reliefs are depicted in the scene of the Massacre of the Innocents, and mothers are seen defending their children in the noble attitudes of classical statues. The picturesque costume of the sixteenth century has given way to Greco-Roman drapery.

One of the merits of these groups at Chartres is the historical account of French sculpture that they provide. Work started up again in 1610, after a long interruption, due to the disastrous events at the end of the sixteenth century. Thomas Boudin was summoned from Paris and commissioned to represent several scenes from the gospels, notably the Temptation, the Transfiguration, the Resurrection and the Pilgrimage to Emmaüs. His work was vigorous, but lacked refinement. His figures are massive, their hair and beards cascade in exuberant ringlets, their drapery, caught in the wind, often twists and curls[2]. In the Transfiguration scene Michaelangelo's Moses can be recognised, almost overwhelmed by the mass of hair and beard, with no trace of nobility left to him. France had to learn the lessons of proportion and taste once more.

It was only seventy years later that sculpture reappeared in the ambulatory. No less than two hundred statues were required for this great project, which was undertaken in 1681 and was completed, in the last year of the reign of Louis XIV, in

140. Jean de Beauce's spire.

1. Other sculptors, contemporaries of Jean Soulas have completed the story of the Virgin, her Death and her Assumption in the first bays on the northern side without any particular emphasis.
2. For exemple, Christ's drapery in the Resurrection scene.

1715[3]. Jean de Dieu d'Arles, Pierre Legros, Tuby le Jeune and Simon Mazières were the names of the sculptors summoned in turn to Chartres.

There is a strange contrast between the homely style of Jean Soulas and the elaborate style which originated in Rome during the seventeenth century. The purest Italian tradition is demonstrated by the Christ attached to the lower column of Saint Praxède, together with the dead Christ, stretched out on the ground, his upper half resting on his Mother's knees, while Rubens' influence may be seen in the Christ on the Cross, raised up by ropes.

In the eighteenth century the canons wanted to complete the decoration of the choir with yet another work in honour of Notre-Dame. In 1767 they commissioned an Assumption from Charles-Antoine Bridan, who had formerly studied at the Académie de France in Rome. With arms outstretched, the Virgin, supported by marble clouds and accompanied by angels, rises above the altar which represents her tomb. It is the work of a skilful sculptor obviously inspired by Bernini, but in artistic terms a gulf exists between this Triumphant Virgin, whose sculptural virtuousity the canons so admired and the Virgin of the northern portal, who bows so modestly before her Son !

Once Bridan completed the Assumption his next task was to execute the bas-reliefs destined for the decoration of the choir interior. They also celebrated the Virgin, one of them representing the Council of Ephesus where Mary was proclaimed 'Mother of God' and another Louis XIII, dedicating his kingdom to Notre-Dame with a holy vow. The last bas-relief was completed in 1789.

The series had now come to a close, and the Revolution was about to arrive. A Phrygian bonnet was placed on the head of Bridan's Virgin, but fortunately only a small number of statues and stained glass windows were destroyed. Such is the history of this extraordinary church. With its ten thousand painted or sculpted figures, its populace equalled that of the town.

French genius is here revealed in all its purity, for Chartres cathedral is one of the great chapters of French history. Foreign influences, still apparent in the twelfth century finally disappeared in the thirteenth century[4].

Better than any book, Chartres cathedral resurrects the Middle Ages in France, and brings them literally within our grasp. The past always resembles something of a dream, but at Chartres, history is real and vividly present. The depths of the thought and inspiration of the Middle Ages, generally so elusive, are revealed here in stone. A world of certitude, order and peace confronts the spectator who beholds here the majesty of the divine plan. It shows us humanity purified, and at the same time proposes this as a model. Never was such an effort made to raise the spirit of man. What other period, what other people, could parallel this spiritual triumph ? It is unjust to grant France the genius of proportion alone, when her true genius is of such scope and magnificence.

Chartres cathedral, and all those that followed constitute one of the most beautiful images of the country. We can only reflect with horror upon the fate of France, and of the world, if these sublime monuments, the summits of human achievement, should one day disappear.

3. The last statuettes on the choir-screen buttresses were put in place a little later, in 1727.
4. The window of Saint George, that of Saint Anne carrying the Virgin as a Child and a few figures of seraphim may just qualify : one can sense an imitation of enamels brought back from Constantinople.

Contents

Table of illustrations